The Nutcracker Backstage

The Story and the Magic

Angela Whitehill and William Noble

Princeton Book Company, Publishers

Princeton Book Company, Publishers
614 U.S. Highway 130
Hightstown, New Jersey 08520

A Dance Horizons Book.

Library of Congress Cataloging-in-Publication Data
Whitehill, Angela, 1938–
     The nucracker backstage: the story and the magic / Angela Whitehill and William Noble.
          p. cm.
Includes bibliographical references.
     ISBN 0–87127–264–4 (hardcover)
1. Nutcracker (Choreographic work) I. Noble, William. II. Title.
     GV1790.N8W54 2004
     796.8'42—dc22

                                                          2004047324

Design by Elizabeth Helmetsie

Photo Credits
Amanda McKerrow. Photograph, page 103
American Ballet Theatre. Courtesy Annie Moleski. Photograph by Rosalie O'Connor, pages 87 and 113
Ballet Ensemble of Texas. Photographs by Cathy Vanover, pages 4, 12, 15, 16, 17, 22, 24, 25, 26, 29, 32, 42, 47, 48, 49, 50, 52, 53, 55, 61, 67, 68, 78, 81, 83, 88, 98, 100, 105, 109, 110, 113, 118, and 119
Ballet Tucson. Photographs by Tim Fuller, pages 28 and 115
New Adventures Company. Photographs by Catherine Ashmore, pages 72 and 76
New Jersey Ballet. Photographs by Joseph Schrembri, pages 11, 19, 23, 27, 37, 84, 93, 114, and 115
New York City Ballet. Photographs by Paul Kolnik. Used courtesy of George Balanchine's The Nutcracker™, choreography by George Balanchine© The Balanchine Trust, pages 7, 9, 14, 44, 65, 79, 95, and 96
N.J. Whitehill III. Photographs, pages 107 and 108
Olympic Ballet Theatre. Photographs by Gordon Kirk, jacket and pages 46, 65, 96, and 104
Oregon Ballet Theatre. Page 74
Pacific Northwest Ballet. Photographs by Angela Sterling, pages 18, 20, 36, 38, 51, 69, 70, and 117. Photographs by Matthew Lawrence, pages 35 and 82. Pacific Northwest Ballet archival photographs, pages 13, 21, 37, 58, 62 and 106. The Mouse Family, Pacific Northwest Ballet School dancers, PNB archival photo, page 60
San Diego Civic Youth Ballet. Photographs by Mikki Breining, pages 30 and 33
Tucson Regional Ballet. Photograph by Jon Wolf, page 75
Tutu.com, pages 40 and 41
Vermont Ballet Theater. Photographs by Ralph Carbo, pages 85 and 92
Vineland Regional Dance Company. Photographs by Chris J. Kane, pages 15, 31, 42, 45, 57, 65, 67, 80, and 101
Wendy Whelan. Photographs from her collection, pages 54 and 97

Printed in Singapore   1 2 3 4 5 6

To Alexandra, James, Madeline, Michael and Nataleigh

Contents

Arabian Coffee. Courtesy Ballet Ensemble of Texas. Photograph by Cathy Vanover.

Act Two

Wendy Whelan

I was seven years old when I received, in my Christmas stocking, two tickets to the Louisville Ballet's *The Nutcracker*. Those tickets provided my first experience with ballet as a performing art, for though I had been studying it recreationally since the age of three, I had never seen it arranged into a spectacle with lights, props, sets, costumes and real dancers.

As my mother and I took our seats at a Saturday matinee, I gasped when the house lights went down. I remember my mother giggling, as excited as I was, because she had never seen a real ballet either. During intermission, I rambled down to take a peek over the railing of the orchestra pit. I wanted to see where all the enchanting music was coming from.

Afterwards, my most vivid memory was of Arabian Coffee. With a turquoise harem costume and bejeweled belly button, she stood out, an exotic figure among the confectionery delights of Act Two. I was captivated and wanted to be like her, one day.

The next year, my best friend Liz asked if I wanted to audition with her for children's parts in *The Nutcracker*. Her mother dropped us off at the company's Oak Street studios, and we took our place on a long, wide staircase filled with hopefuls, numbers pinned to our backs. Would we make it, or worse, would one of us make it without the other? Together, we braved the audition and gleefully took home the roles of mice. It was as if we had been handed the keys to a fantastic dream.

I spent my weekends at the studio, which we would come to call "Oak Street," watching the director piece the production together. The sculpted bodies of the company dancers riveted me, and I studied them endlessly. Much of the choreography came to me by watching the rehearsals, and I would practice at home in the family room. Over time, I gained insight into the elements that make up a production: not only dancers but set designers, costume and lighting designers, musicians, stage managers and makeup artists. I couldn't believe that so many different kinds of artists would come together with the single goal of creating a performance.

I became captivated by the backstage world with its juxtapositions and extremes: ratty warmup clothes and colorful beaded costumes; tiny, focused ballerinas next to burly, joke-telling stagehands; the out-of-breath reality of the wings and the realm of the stage where it all looks so effortless. The play of light, between the wings and the stage, can stir up fantastic feelings of energy and emotion. It's a toss-up as to which vantage point is truly better, the wings or the audience.

I have now danced over five hundred performances of *The Nutcracker* and rehearsed many thousands of hours on the fifteen different roles I have performed. In fact, *The Nutcracker* was the first ballet I ever danced with the

Principal Dancer Wendy Whelan as Sugar Plum Fairy with Damian Woetzel as her Cavalier.

• THE NEW YORK CITY BALLET

New York City Ballet when I was an apprentice. Eventually, I was given the opportunity to dance the role of Dewdrop and later my dream role, that of Arabian Coffee for the film version of *George Balanchine's The Nutcracker*.

Mostly now, I dance the part of the Sugar Plum Fairy, the embodiment of serenity and regal graciousness. It took me years to cultivate myself for this leading role. I have had the privilege of working with Balanchine's first Sugar Plum, Maria Tallchief, and she gave me wonderful insights into the ideas behind his choreography. She showed me how to let my partner lead me into every step and guide me as if we were ballroom dancing together (an idea that is vital to many of Balanchine's ballets) and to approach the role as if I were a jewel or a flower that my partner is presenting to the audience. Over time, I've developed a coterie of visual ideas that I can call upon; lovely, personal images that I make use of often.

Frequently, I appear as a guest artist and have enjoyed taking part in many different productions over the years. I travel to big cities and small towns and am always happy to meet the young dancers in these places. Watching them, I am reminded of myself at their age and of how important it was for me as a young girl in Louisville to see guest artists such as Patricia McBride, Mikhail Baryshnikov, Merrill Ashley and Sean Lavery when they came to town. It's hard to overstate how essential it was to my development to have observed them.

It was by working on *Nutcracker* that I began to understand the level of commitment involved in being a creative artist. It was where I learned about the beauty of process and where I vowed to devote myself to the art of ballet. As a child, I remember taking a small piece of rosin from "Oak Street" as a souvenir. I still have it, and it amazes me to think that I might have known back then what it would mean to me now.

The Story

The Nutcracker

Many years ago in a small German village, Mayor Stahlbaum and his wife are giving a Christmas party, and the house buzzes with excitement. Their children, Clara and Fritz, try to peek into the parlor. The door majestically opens, and there, in the corner of the room, stands a huge Christmas tree surrounded with brightly packaged presents.

The children try to peek through the door. • NEW JERSEY BALLET

The girls are enchanted by their beautiful china dolls.

"Come, children," the Mayor motions them in, "it's time for our guests to arrive." He picks up Clara and holds her high above his head. "You shall place the star and light the tree." He carries her to put the star at the top. Then they step back to admire what she has done.

Soon, the guests begin to arrive. Children and adults greet one another in the high spirits of the season. There is a present for everyone under the tree, and it wouldn't do to wait another moment before opening them. "Look, look!" the children shout, paper and ribbons flying through the air. The boys show off toy drums, trumpets, toy soldiers and a wooden hobby-horse while the girls coo over beautiful china dolls, complete with prams and beds.

"Welcome to our home at this wonderful Christmas season," the Mayor beams to all.

Suddenly, the front door flies open, and a cold wind rushes across the revelers. There stands the mysterious Dr. Drosselmeyer, accompanied by his handsome young nephew.

The mysterious Dr. Drosselmeyer, accompanied by his handsome young nephew.
• PACIFIC NORTHWEST BALLET

"Godfather!" gasps Clara, and she rushes into his arms.

"My child, how you are growing up!" he exclaims, enveloping her in his purple and black cape. His wild white hair and black eye patch make him a strange figure indeed. "I would like to introduce you to my nephew," he says. The young man bows low and kisses Clara's hand.

"I have brought puppets," Drosselmeyer says. At his signal, two large boxes are rolled in. "Open!" Drosselmeyer commands, and lifts out two life-sized dolls: a beautiful ballerina and a harlequin in a suit of brightly colored diamonds. Carefully, his nephew winds them up. First the ballerina dances and spins, throwing kisses to the children. Then, the harlequin leaps and turns, bowing to his ballerina.

When the dancing is finished, Drosselmeyer turns to Clara. "For you, my dear, I have a special gift," and places a brightly painted nutcracker doll in her hands.

"Godfather!" gasps Clara, and she rushes into his arms.

• THE NEW YORK CITY BALLET

"Open!" Drosselmeyer commands, and lifts out two life-sized dolls.

• VINELAND REGIONAL DANCE COMPANY

"For you, my dear, I have a special gift," and he places a brightly painted nutcracker doll in her hands.

• BALLET ENSEMBLE OF TEXAS

"He's magical, oh thank you. . . ." • BALLET ENSEMBLE OF TEXAS

"I want one!" stamps Fritz,
grabbing the toy from Clara...
• BALLET ENSEMBLE OF TEXAS

Clara says breathlessly, "He's—he's magical, oh thank you. . . ."

"I want one!" stamps Fritz, grabbing the toy from Clara, but as he

starts to run off, the nutcracker slips from his hands and falls, cracking

its jaw.

Dr. Drosselmeyer gently sets the broken toy's jaw.

• PACIFIC NORTHWEST BALLET

"Ohhh. . . ." Clara wails, but Dr. Drosselmeyer uses a handkerchief and gently sets the broken toy's jaw. Then he places it in one of the children's doll beds.

"It will be better in the morning," Drosselmeyer soothes, and within moments the party resumes in earnest.

Late that night, after the guests have left and everyone has gone to bed, Clara creeps down the stairs to find her nutcracker. As she reaches him, the big Grandfather clock begins to strike the midnight hour. *Bong . . . bong . . . bong . . .* There! Peering at her over the clock is Dr. Drosselmeyer. . . .

She can tell he is an evil, ugly creature, a Mouse King, no less!

• PACIFIC NORTHWEST BALLET

And the Christmas tree begins to grow . . . the furniture in the room begins to grow . . . and the great room window begins to grow . . . and the fireplace begins to grow . . . even the doll's bed begins to grow. . . .

"Ohhh!" Clara gasps as a mouse suddenly appears, followed by another mouse . . . and still another. . . . She leaps onto the couch, clutching her beloved nutcracker. But these are not ordinary mice: some are as tall as she is! And the one in the middle has three heads, and on each head is a shiny gold crown. She could tell he is an evil, ugly creature, a Mouse King, no less!

Crash! Boom! Out of one of the toy boxes marches a squad of toy soldiers, led by a rabbit—and like the mice they are as tall as Clara.

And who follows them? Her nutcracker, now grown into life size. A terrible battle begins—mice against soldiers, Mouse King against Nutcracker. Guns pop, cannons boom, swords clash. . . . Clara jumps onto the doll's bed for safety.

Out of one of the toy boxes marches a squad of toy soldiers. . . .

• PACIFIC NORTHWEST BALLET

A terrible battle begins—mice against soldiers, Mouse King against Nutcracker.

• PACIFIC NORTHWEST BALLET

The dreadful mice seem to be winning, and then the Nutcracker loses his sword. Clara fears for his safety. She slips off her shoe and throws it at the Mouse King, hitting him in the face.

Down he goes, striking the floor in a lump as his mouse soldiers surround his lifeless body. One little mouse waves the white flag of surrender.

"You saved my life!" the Nutcracker exclaims to Clara, and as she watches in amazement, he turns into a handsome prince, looking very much like her godfather's handsome nephew.

"Come with me," the Prince urges, "I'll show you the wonders of my kingdom." She takes his hand, and he guides her to the window, leading her out to an enchanted snow forest where the falling snowflakes look like tiny dancing fairies. They find the Snow Queen and her Cavalier dancing among the falling snow. As the Cavalier gently lifts the Snow Queen high above the ground, she summons a fantasy sleigh for Clara and the Prince.

"I am taking you to my Kingdom of Sweets," says the Prince, "but first, we must fly past the angels," and in the flash of an instant a chorus

As the Cavalier gently lifts the Snow Queen high above the ground, she summons a fantasy sleigh for Clara and the Prince.
• BALLET ENSEMBLE OF TEXAS

of little angels appears, dressed in shimmering white with brightly colored wings and halos. Some pluck tiny harps and play silver flutes. Their music is beautiful.

Soon, they arrive at the Palace of Sweets where the Sugar Plum Fairy and her Bonbon attendants greet them. "Tell me how you have come here," the Sugar Plum Fairy asks, and the Prince reenacts his battle

The Sugar Plum Fairy places a crown on Clara's head. . . .

with the mice and Mouse King, emphasizing Clara's bravery and their narrow escape.

"My loyal subjects will dance for you," the Sugar Plum Fairy says. She places a crown on Clara's head and leads them to a pair of golden thrones. She royally claps her hands.

An elaborate ceremony with exotic dancers from faraway lands begins, all bringing luscious, delectable sweets and spices. First, to the sounds of Spain, there's Chocolate, and three *señors* and their *señoritas* twirl on stage, costumed in dark and mysterious colors.

Next comes Tea, and out of a teapot jump a pair of Chinese dancers dressed in silk trousers, bright jackets and coolie hats. They are joined by a jeweled dragon breathing fire.

Then, the lights dim as a flute plays a mysterious dance . . . here comes Coffee, four men dressed in flowing harem pants with armbands who carry a beautiful woman on a golden throne. She is an Arabian Princess.

Arabian Coffee, dressed in silk and bejeweled pants, with a band of jewels around her head. . . .
• BALLET ENSEMBLE OF TEXAS

Gently, they put her down, she steps onto the stage, her attendants

bowing. She captivates Clara with a long, sensuous dance, bending and

sweeping in deep movements. Dressed in silk and bejeweled pants, with

a band of jewels around her head, her eyes flash.

*Cossack dancers appear, leaping
and spinning in front of them. . . .*
• BALLET ENSEMBLE OF TEXAS

Energetic Cossack dancers appear, leaping and spinning in front of them in bright Russian costumes. They jump high in the air, legs spread wide, then landing close to the floor in a deep knee bend, kicking their legs and crossing their arms. They jump over one another and finish with daring back flips. Clara, amazed, claps her hands in joy.

Next frolic three shepherdesses, or Mirlitons, playing their delicate reed flutes, tiny lambs bounding around them.

For Clara, it is a cornucopia of delights. She sits transfixed. "Look!" points the Prince, and a huge woman, as tall as a cherry tree, lumbers on stage, carrying a plumed fan. It is Mother Ginger, or Bonbon, and she has orange hair, big red lips, and wears a rainbow-colored crinoline—out of which her many children, French polichinelle dolls, will mischievously emerge and begin to dance.

Soon, the stage fills with all the flowers of the Kingdom, led by a sparkling Dewdrop. They, too, dance for Clara and her Prince.

And last, the Sugar Plum Fairy and her Cavalier take center stage and perform an exquisite *pas de deux* while all in attendance watch enraptured. When she is finished, Sugar Plum turns to Clara and announces, "Now, we will all dance!" She nods at Coffee, Tea, Chocolate, the Mirlitons and Dewdrop and soon the stage is filled with swirling dancers.

Alas, it becomes time for Clara to leave her Nutcracker Prince and the Kingdom of Sweets. As if by magic, the sleigh appears, Clara steps aboard, and as all the dancers wave their good-byes, Clara is whisked off into the starlit sky, waving sadly to her Prince . . . her sleigh gently floating on. . . .

"Look!" points the Prince, and a woman as tall as a cherry tree lumbers on stage . . . she wears a rainbow-colored crinoline—out of which her many children, the polichinelles, will mischievously emerge. . . .
• NEW JERSEY BALLET

27

As morning comes, Clara awakens to find herself in her own bed, still clutching her nutcracker.

• BALLET TUCSON

And she feels the soft touch of her mother's hand and senses her mother bending over her and kissing her. She reaches to pull up her covers as her mother quietly moves away. As morning comes, Clara awakens to find herself in her own bed, still clutching her nutcracker.

It has been a beautiful dream.

Act One

Clara and her Prince

Many years ago in a small German village, Mayor Stahlbaum and his wife are giving a Christmas party. . . . Their children, Clara and Fritz, try to peek into the parlor. . . .

I
t happens in early fall, as autumn chill invades and days begin to shorten, a notice goes up on the ballet studio bulletin board: NUTCRACKER AUDITIONS!

The annual ballet rite, *The Nutcracker*, has begun in hundreds of studios and company rehearsal halls across America. It is the time when ballet students arrive for class, read the audition notice and begin to imagine performing in one of the *Nutcracker* roles. As they stand in neat leotards, hair carefully brushed into the obligatory bun, their excitement is manifest. Looks of determination cross the children's faces. "Well, someday, I am going to dance *Clara!*" says one tiny girl.

Clara! The leading role every young ballet student dreams to dance, and for many it is the culmination of months and years of arduous ballet training. But talent beyond dance skill is often considered. "It's not necessarily the best dancer we choose for Clara," says Bruce Marks, former artistic director of Boston Ballet. "We look for a child who embodies the innocence of the character, a child who can act. And size is a major factor, too: we want a child who will fit into the costume."

Clara is not the universal name for this role because some companies, through tradition, call their heroine *Marie*. Marie, not Clara, is commonly used in *Nutcrackers* throughout Russia, particularly in the Bolshoi and Kirov Ballet Companies. Part of the reason lies in the fact that E.T.A. Hoffman's original version of the story (1816) was, and is, extremely popular throughout Russia, and Marie is the main character's name. Yet the Frenchman Marius Petipa, choreographer of the original *Nutcracker*, did not speak Russian well. According the late George Balanchine, the great choreographer and artistic director of the New York City Ballet, ". . . when Petipa tried to speak Russian, he came up with all kinds of inadvertent words." Naturally, Petipa turned to French

Whether her name is Clara (as in some productions) or Marie (as in others), she embodies the innocence of the character.
• VINELAND REGIONAL DANCE COMPANY

Facing page: Dancers check the cast list at San Diego Civic Youth Ballet.

The first performance of *The Nutcracker* was December 18, 1892.

Houston's American Academy of Dance uses technology to post the cast list. "Our auditions take place on a Saturday and Sunday, and we decide on final casting by Wednesday," says Artistic Director Angela Jackson. "By two-thirty p.m. on Thursday, we post the list on our web site. This way any fears or tears are in the privacy of the child's home rather than in our studio lobby in front of peers, other parents and teachers."

Clara and the Nutcracker Prince must fit one another and be in proportion to the rest of the cast.

literature for his story source, and found a version by Alexandre Dumas (the father) who called his heroine "Clara." It was likely he felt more comfortable creating his work in French and adhering to the Dumas storyline.

In the United States, George Balanchine, perhaps because of his Russian training, used Marie in his *Nutcracker,* and American companies adopting his choreography, such as the New York City Ballet, Atlanta Ballet, Miami City Ballet and Pittsburgh Ballet, also call their lead Marie. But Clara or Marie, the role remains the same.

It all starts with the audition process, which will become a part of a dancer's life year after year. Auditions for *Nutcracker* are usually held in late September. Announcements appear on dance studio and dance boutique bulletin boards, in the arts calendars of local newspapers and on local radio stations. Audition times are set for each group of characters, such as *Angels:* 2 P.M., *Children:* 3:30 P.M., *Soldiers:* 5:00 P.M.; then come age and experience requirements, such as: "Angels must be on pointe" "Children level 3 or higher." Often, height limitations are also specified for individual characters. For example, the mice must be tiny and quick because the role calls for the characters to dart around Clara as she begins to dream in the transformation scene. Or the Mouse King must be extra large so the character can seem to tower ferociously over those around him, providing credibility for the role.

Even Clara and her Prince must fit one another (a Clara four inches taller than her Prince simply wouldn't do!) and they both must be in proportion to the rest of the cast. In some ballet companies, the height requirements are less

Dancers auditioning, numbers pinned to the front of their leotards, at the San Diego Civic Youth Ballet.

"The first day we audition the dancers from our own school," says Sharon Story, director of the Center for Dance Education at the Atlanta Ballet. "It's easier to work with the children we know, but we also want to give children from other schools a chance, too. So, on the second day, we see children from the other schools."

stringent than in others; for example, in Pacific Northwest Ballet, the professional dancers tend to be taller, so there is latitude in what will be acceptable.

Audition day arrives, and young dancers pile into the rehearsal studio, excited yet understanding above all else that how they conduct themselves from here on will bear on the role they ultimately get.

Sharon Story makes it seem like a simple day's work, but it's much more than that. Before they're through with auditions, major ballet companies such as the Atlanta Ballet, Pacific Northwest Ballet, or the New York City Ballet will look at from six to eight hundred children, and then casting choices must be made! "It's not easy," many an artistic director will remark with understatement because once the cast is assembled, the *real* work begins.

For many children the *Nutcracker* experience will be their first exposure to the audition process, one that will be repeated at every stage of a dance career.

Helen Starr, Associate Director of the Louisville Ballet says: "children cannot be evaluated when their parents are looking in windows or peering through doors. We need total control while they are with us." At many ballet companies, even the children's ballet teachers are not allowed to watch the auditions, so no favoritism can be shown. Boston Ballet, for example, limits in-studio personnel to the artistic director, the company's "children's rehearsal teacher" and the costumer.

"At the end of the audition, I take the children who are not getting cast into a separate room and talk with them," says Sharon Story. "I explain that the reason they haven't been chosen is not necessarily because of how they dance but that we are looking for a certain height or costume size." She urges them to keep dancing and will welcome them for the following year's *Nutcracker* auditions.

Then, she gathers together the children who have been chosen. "We let them know which parts they will be dancing, when rehearsals will be and the time commitment we will expect from them," she adds. "Then I urge them to be kind to their less fortunate auditioning friends."

Its significance cannot be overemphasized. In the words of the late Alexander Bennett, founder and Artistic Director of the Scottish-American Ballet, "It's never too early to get started."

First, the children are given a number to pin to the front of leotards on girls or tee shirts on boys. "Please wait outside the studio," the auditioner says, telling them they will be called inside by number groups. "Don't worry, we'll see all of you."

Then, parents are politely informed they should wait outside the studio, that the audition process will be "closed." Parents often make their children nervous or worse: they interfere.

"Line up over here," the auditioner points, "tallest to the left." Then the auditioner will perform a simple combination of steps, such as *glissade, jeté, pas de bourrée, pas de chat* or simple runs across the floor, and asks the children—in groups of five or ten—to duplicate the combination. When each group has completed the combination, they will be asked to repeat it . . . and repeat it, often six or eight times, until the auditioner feels comfortable making the right selections. The next group of children will then be called into the studio and go through the same process, and the next group after that until all have been seen. Then comes the moment of decision, and the auditioner knows there will be unavoidable peaks and valleys of elation and disappointment to deal with.

The children are given a thick packet of information listing rehearsal times, costume requirements and performance etiquette, such as when they are expected at the theater, what to bring with them (tights, shoes, leotard), what

not to bring (food, drinks, toys, chewing gum) and studio pick-up and drop-off procedures. "The most important thing a parent can do is read all the information, understand it and make the commitment to help turn *Nutcracker* into a truly wonderful experience for their child," Sharon Story underscores.

Every company will cast one Clara (or Marie) and at least one understudy, though some will even cast more of both. In the Sacramento (California) Ballet, former artistic director and founder Barbara Crockett usually chooses two Claras and two understudies. In the New York City Ballet, there are five separate casts with five Maries and understudies.

"Our Clara was always a young teenager, a dancer whose pointe work was strong but who was small so she looked like a child," says Joseph Carow, former director of the New Jersey Ballet. "I imagine her as a young girl about to fall in love for the first time. The *pas de deux* after the mouse fight scene is that tentative recognition of what romance might be like."

In the New York City Ballet Marie is a child, an exuberant, fun-loving girl enchanted with her new nutcracker toy and ready to get her brother Fritz in trouble.

Artistic directors have their own visions of how Clara should look and dance, of course. The traditional *Nutcracker* is set in the late nineteenth century, so the traditional Clara should embody the Victorian child, as that artistic director envisions her.

One thing that is common to all the Claras or Maries no matter the company, no matter the number of *Nutcracker* performances: the role requires a serious commitment involving many hours of rehearsals. Clara is the central character in the ballet, and she rarely leaves the stage. It is *her* story.

Many productions "fly" Clara and her Prince out of the Land of Snow, and in the finale, she "flies" away from the Land of Sweets. There will be rehearsals in the sleigh or balloon, rehearsals on the moving doll bed (now, of course, life-sized), there will be mime rehearsals with the Prince and the Sugar Plum Fairy so they learn to act, as well as dance, their roles. There will even be rehearsals where Clara and her Prince learn to sit quietly on their thrones in Act Two!

Every evening before a performance Clara will set her hair into ringlets or sausage curls (unless the director prefers a hair piece), and it's not unusual to see a young dancer going to school in "hair rags" (the Victorian way of making curls) as a badge of honor.

Artistic directors have individual visions about Clara's Prince, as well. In the Balanchine version, the Prince is a child about the same age and height as Marie. He, too, will go through the audition process and should be a very good actor. He must explain clearly to the Sugar Plum Fairy (through mime) why and how he has chosen to bring Clara to the Kingdom of Sweets. His mime section at the beginning of Act Two is a major part of his role and one that can bring applause for his solo performance.

In the *Nutcracker* versions in which Clara is a teenager, the prince must have serious dance training and be able to partner her in the *pas de deux* after she has saved him from the Mouse King. Often, the prince is a young-looking professional dancer from the company, not someone chosen at the children's auditions. He is the same dancer who dances the part of Dr. Drosselmeyer's handsome nephew.

As the children emerge from the studio, the auditions concluded, their roles assigned, the tiny girl who wanted to be Clara touches her friend on the shoulder. "It'll be so much fun, I won't mind being Clara's friend this year."

Clara and the Nutcracker Prince in their Act One pas de deux.
• NEW JERSEY BALLET

Party children's ringlets, gathered in ribbons.
• PACIFIC NORTHWEST BALLET

Party Children

Soon, the guests begin to arrive. Children and adults greet one another in the high spirits of the season. . . .

The auditions are over, casting is posted, information packets have been handed out and rehearsals have been scheduled. *Nutcracker* season is in full swing.

A set of children has been chosen to perform in the opening party scene, and usually, because the roles can be fairly demanding, those children have had at least one year of experience in lesser *Nutcracker* roles, such as mice or angels. These children must embody the Victorian spirit of the *Nutcracker* story, projecting sweetness and innocence, behaving politely and respecting adults and peers.

The age of the dancer is sometimes of less concern than physical size. For many directors, an older child is easier to work with. A tiny fourteen-year-old understands more than the same-sized ten-year-old and will usually handle a role more comfortably. But the costumes themselves also play significant parts. When a company tours and fills in with local dancers, there is simply no time to alter costumes in each city. When the Atlanta Ballet touring company auditioned for its *Nutcracker* party scene, Joanne Lee, the children's ballet mistress, would have—right there!—the smallest and largest children's costumes. And during the audition process, she would measure those initially chosen for girth and height; the dancers who fit her costumes would be finally accepted. There really was little choice.

Costuming in the overall *Nutcracker* performance, as well as in the party scene, is equally as important. The extravagance of the storyline coupled with the size of the cast and the scenes of fantasy and magic make it a thoroughly involving, and expensive, experience from beginning to end. For example, when the Atlanta Ballet danced the Balanchine version of *Nutcracker,* there were 1,200 individual costume pieces to account for and use in every performance!

Paul McCrea, Associate Artistic Director of New Jersey Ballet remembers six-year-old David who auditioned to dance as a clown in Act Two. "He was the perfect child to play the youngest and very cute clown," he recalls. "He did a wonderful job during the six weeks of rehearsal, but on opening night he took one look at the hat he had to wear and flatly refused to go on stage. Whether it was a costume issue or simple stage fright, we'll never know," he laughs, "but it was a difficult beginning to what now appears to be a budding career. This year he's dancing our Sugar Plum Cavalier!"

Facing page: Party children, dressed as Victorians
• PACIFIC NORTHWEST BALLET

A classical tutu is a work of art.

What of the dancer's signature costume piece—the tutu? A single tutu for Sugar Plum Fairy or Snow Queen can cost as much as four thousand dollars! Up to fifty separate pieces of fabric can go into the construction of a classical tutu—before the trimmings and decorations are applied. In the costume shop at London's Royal Ballet, it's commonly believed that the most experienced seamstress will need about fourteen hours to complete a single, basic (unadorned) tutu, while a less experienced seamstress might take more than twenty hours for the same job.

Seamstresses spend hours on the construction of a tutu.

Of course, with this kind of investment, a ballet company needs a professional staff to care for the costumes. Even the smallest company must have a designer, a costumer, seamstresses, sewers, a wardrobe mistress or master, dressers and menders.

Once the company begins to rehearse, each dressing room will be assigned a dresser. In a large professional company like the Boston Ballet, these men and women will be part of the theater's union crew. In smaller companies

This is the way costume work is assigned:

Designer: conceives and draws the costumes with notations on construction, buys fabric, oversees pattern choices, cutting, and the finished product.

Costumer: cuts costume pieces, hires staff, oversees construction and final decoration and finish of the costumes; makes shipping, packing and storage plans when on tour.

Wardrobe mistress/master: helps with the construction, storage and care of the costumes, hires the dressers, oversees the steaming, ironing and distribution of the costumes, is responsible for the maintenance of the costumes during the run of the ballet, decides when the costumes need cleaning and launders tights and other small items between shows.

Seamstress: works on the construction of the costume.

Sewer: works on the trim, affixes the final hook and eye, helps keep track of the layers of net on the tutu skirt.

A quick backstage repair for an angel.
• VINELAND REGIONAL DANCE COMPANY

Dancers help each other fasten their costumes. • BALLET ENSEMBLE OF TEXAS

such as Olympic (Washington) Ballet or Michigan Classic Ballet, dressers are usually volunteers. But whatever the size of the company, the requirements for a dresser are the same: infinite patience, particularly for quick changes, hand and finger dexterity (for fastening rows of hooks and eyes), an ability to see in

the backstage darkness, to always carry two threaded needles (one white, one black) for quick backstage repairs and a pair of sharp scissors to trim stray threads.

In larger companies, such as the Atlanta Ballet, there are menders on each side of the stage for minor, on-the-spot repairs, and they move to the wardrobe department to do larger repairs when the company is between performances.

Many companies, especially during *Nutcracker* season, rely upon volunteer parents to help with the children's costumes, and it can be a formidable responsibility. For example, in the party scene, as guest families arrive at the Stahlbaum's house, they wear coats, hats, scarves and mittens (remember, it's Christmastime and the weather outside is wintry). Each character's outerwear must be carefully taken and piled backstage so it can be retrieved. One little child may have a coat, muff, gloves, a bonnet and scarf—five pieces for one child of one family, and there may be four or five children in *each* family, and there may be ten *other* families with more than one child. . . . Soon the number of costume pieces to be accounted for will be in the hundreds! And at the conclusion of the scene, each costume piece must be returned to the right character as they leave the party. All of this is done on stage, smoothly, naturally and elegantly—in full view of the audience.

With so many characters coming and going on stage and the huge number of costumes, there are bound to be occasional rips and tears. Most companies station several people in the wings to do immediate mending.

Sometimes things simply happen that no one can foresee. A volunteer parent recalls standing in the wings during Colorado Ballet's *Nutcracker*. "It had been one of the coldest winters people in Denver could recall," she said, "and most dancers wore lots of leg warmers offstage. I was standing with the costumer during the performance when, to our surprise, we saw that one of the dancers on stage had forgotten to remove her red leg warmers! It took two of us to restrain the costumer from running on stage and physically removing them."

"I remember three wonderful Spanish costumes in sparkling copper chiffon, each with layers upon layers of sequin-edged ruffles on the skirts," remembers a former costumer for the Atlanta Ballet. "The bodices were constructed with bone and underlined with sections topped with a sequined ruffle over the shoulder. At dress rehearsal the dancers were brilliant until the last *jeté* (lift). There was the searing sound of ripping fabric, and all three Spanish dancers grabbed the back of their costumes. All at the same time the fabric on the hook and eye tapes had ripped and disintegrated. As their partners held on to the back of their bodices, they all took a quick bow and ran offstage where the dressers quickly took the costumes to be repaired before the finale.

Each child must remember to bring all his props on stage.
• THE NEW YORK CITY BALLET

While children are not as hard on costumes as the production's professional dancers (who perform the snow scene and all the Act Two characters), there are still many costume pieces to remember. The party girls wear pantaloons, petticoats, dresses, hair ribbons and sometimes pinafores or special lace collars as well as outer clothes. Usually, tights and shoes are supplied by the

dancers. Their hair must be set each night, brushed out and curled before every performance.

The boys' costumes aren't quite as demanding, yet the numbers can multiply: pants, socks, shorts, coats, vests, jackets, jabeaux and shoes, coat, muffler, gloves and hat at the very least. And there is more. Each child must remember to pick up his or her props, like the gift he or she will carry to the party, where it will be put under the tree, the gift he or she will receive at the party and where on the backstage prop table that gift will be returned at the conclusion of the scene. Each child does not leave the stage area until the gifts have been returned to the prop table in the appropriate place.

The dancing and acting the children do in each *Nutcracker* production has the same *intent* but rarely the same *steps* because every production will bear the individual stamp of the artistic director or choreographer, who has a particular image he or she wishes to create. In the New Jersey Ballet, for instance, the party children girls dance on pointe, while in other companies, like the Louisville Ballet, the children will be younger and less sophisticated.

Whatever the choreography, the children have much to learn and much to retain. They must remember all their steps, they must remember where they are on stage in relation to the other cast members, and that there is an audience behind those blinding lights.

They must remember, above all else, that they are performers who are creating a performance!

Even the Artistic Director, Maxine Chapman, helps to get the dancers ready.
• VINELAND REGIONAL DANCE COMPANY

Dr. Drosselmeyer and Party Parents

Soon, the guests begin to arrive. "Welcome to our home at this wonderful Christmas season," the Mayor beams. . . . Suddenly the door flies open. . . . There stands the mysterious Dr. Drosslemeyer. . . .

*I*t is your first *Nutcracker* as a parent. Your child has been chosen to be a party child, and you are in the initial parents' meeting. Around you, the talk is of commitment and rehearsals, large portions of time spent on behalf of your child, driving your child or waiting for your child, while the annual production is put together. In addition, many parents are asked to share in the excitement of the production by contributing their time in other ways. But, listening carefully, you'll also discover something else: not all volunteer parents work as drivers or chaperones or seamstresses. Some actually perform! A lucky few might actually be in the production as "party parents."

Most small and a few larger companies need volunteers for every imaginable specialty backstage: stagehands, electricians, painters, seamstresses, program stuffers, ushers, boutique salespeople, chaperones, coat checkers and even babysitters. Then, there are those who will work with the dancers: makeup artists, hair stylists, backstage chaperones, rehearsal assistants. At the Boston Ballet, professional staff is hired to help the children with their hair, make-up, dressing, arrival and departure from the theater, but parents are asked to help in the lobby boutique.

Sometimes, volunteering can take on major proportions. At Northern Ballet Theatre (New Hampshire), Artistic Director Doreen Cafferella was preparing a new *Nutcracker* production and invited volunteers to come to a seminar months before the season to learn tutu-making. Each volunteer was asked to bring a sewing machine, scissors, pins, paper for drawing patterns, and to expect to work for twenty hours over a single weekend. Ten people came, and by the end of the weekend each had made a classical tutu skirt, a long romantic skirt and a ten-piece boned bodice for use with either skirt. It was

Volunteers have many talents.
• BALLET ENSEMBLE OF TEXAS

Facing page: Fathers get a chance to dance, too.
• OLYMPIC BALLET THEATRE

"The dedication of the parents directly affects the outcome of the continuing magic, year after year: it's a group effort," insists Sharon Story of the Atlanta Ballet.

Melissa Framiglio, formerly a principal dancer with Louisville Ballet remembers her first *Nutcracker*. "My mom sewed costumes, my dad built scenery and my sister painted it. I got to help by pinning snowflakes on the curtain. The problem was I was really tiny so that all the snowflakes were only four-and-a-half feet high on the curtain!"

Volunteers even get a chance to wear a tutu . . . just for adjustments!

• BALLET ENSEMBLE OF TEXAS

clearly a winning situation: Northern Ballet Theatre now had professional tutus, and the tutu-makers had learned a skill they could use again and again.

Not every company welcomes parents on stage. In fact, not every company uses children in the opening party scene; at American Ballet Theatre and New York City Ballet, the party-goers are all professional company dancers.

Party parents aren't the only performing roles adults and non-dancers can fill. Maids, mice, Dr. Drosselmeyer and even his nephew can sometimes be played by those outside the *Nutcracker* company. At Boston Ballet, the Mouse King was performed by a young company member who was one day prevented by a snowstorm from getting to the theater. Founding director E. Virginia Williams sought out six-foot five-inch Arthur Leeth, a new apprentice with the company who agreed to do the role, but on his terms. "I decided," he remembers, "to do it all on pointe. I'd always wanted to dance on pointe and had been taking a few classes in pointe shoes." When he came off stage, the director was waiting for him, and he was sure he would be fired. But no. "You will do that part from now on. And don't fall off pointe!" she said. For years after, the Mouse King at Boston Ballet was danced by a male dancer on pointe.

For party parents, it can be an exciting time. Imagine going to an elegant party every evening, dressed in a gorgeous gown or suave Victorian evening suit, accompanied by four or five children. Of course the children will be beautifully behaved because they've been taught the stringent etiquette and behavior standards of the Victorian child.

Dr. Drosselmeyer as a magician • BALLET ENSEMBLE OF TEXAS

Real-life mother and daughter Joyce and Julie Stahl played those roles in Princeton Ballet's Nutcracker.

There are those who have spent years relishing the role of party parent. Joyce Stahl, who had three dancing daughters, is one of them. Every year as the Princeton (New Jersey) Ballet's *Nutcracker* season came along, she would spend much of the fall in the studio and several weeks after that in the

theater. One year, when the company was seeking party parents, she thought "why not me?" She performed as a Princeton Ballet party parent for twenty-five years, and says, "It was a wonderful experience for all of us." Now, years later, Joyce lives in Key West, Florida. *Nutcracker* season is coming on, and she is nostalgic. "I'm hoping to bring a company to Key West. Maybe I'll get to dance Mrs. Stahlbaum again!"

One of the most coveted adult roles is that of Dr. Drosselmeyer, Clara's strange, mystical godfather. He appears early in Act One, stays through scene two and usually appears again at the end of Act Two, often dominating events on stage. The role requires someone with acting ability because the character is a catalyst for events, and his actions must move the story along. Here is an opportunity for a family member, especially if the company is small, to be a major part of the production. An interested father or grandfather just might be the right person. (In some of the larger companies, the role is almost

The mysterious Dr. Drosselmeyer • PACIFIC NORTHWEST BALLET

always filled by a retired dancer or professional actor.) Dr. Drosselmeyer is as much a fixture in a *Nutcracker* production as Clara and Sugar Plum Fairy.

So, it may not be unusual to hear one of the little mice turn to a polichinelle and say, "Grandpa's going to be here, too! He's Dr. Drosselmeyer."

Keith Dunn, a private detective in real life, has been performing Drosselmeyer for five years with the Vineland Ballet (New Jersey). "I started with the company years ago," he says. Then he went into military service and toured with the Bob Hope show, entertaining the troops. "That's when performing got into my blood. I sing as well as act, and I love to be on stage." When he came home he was asked to take his niece to a *Nutcracker* audition, and Maxine Chapman, the Artistic Director, made him a butler at the party. When the role of Drosselmeyer became available the following year, he made it his own. "At first I thought my buddies might give me grief, but actually I think they really respect me now. I have to be in good shape, because I have to lift Clara and the life-size puppets. I never know who they will be until the first rehearsal. Will they be tiny or tall? A sylph or on the heavy side? I have to be ready."

Scurrying, Scary Mice

"Ohhh. . . ! Clara gasps as a mouse suddenly appears, followed by another mouse . . . and still another. She leaps onto the couch, clutching her beloved nutcracker. . . .

I t is early Christmas morning, dark and still in the Stahlbaum house, and the children are sleeping peacefully. Party-goers have left, and Mayor Stahlbaum and his wife are gently snoring in their beds. In the quiet, darkened Stahlbaum living room, nothing moves, nothing happens . . . but then, a tiny mouse scurries from under the Christmas tree, sniffing for crumbs . . . then another mouse appears, then still another and another until the stage is filled with skipping, scurrying, sniffing creatures.

Clara appears on the stairs. She's been worrying about her injured nutcracker and unable to sleep. As she creeps down, there are strange little creatures dashing about where a little while ago people were singing Christmas songs, opening presents and playing games! She stands transfixed, as the mice continue to scurry, and dramatic transition from reality to fantasy blossoms into Clara's *Nutcracker* dream.

It is a moment the audience savors. "How *old* are those mice?" a first-time *Nutcracker*-goer might ask. They are such tiny, adorable characters on stage, one wonders if, in spite of their charm, the dancers are simply too young to understand performance demands at this formal level.

Madeline Culpo Cantrella, Artistic Director of the Albany-Berkshire Ballet (New York) thinks so. "They seem to sneak in at four and five years old," she says, "though we believe six to eight years old is where they should begin. Even then, there are some six year olds who aren't ready for the demands of auditioning and performing." Still, the very young dancers seem to be welcomed and cast in more than a few places. In New England (Connecticut) Ballet Company's *Nutcracker,* there are two sets of mice, tiny children aged four and five, and the rest, nine years old and older, who dance in the fight

A tiny mouse scampers from under the Christmas tree.
• BALLET ENSEMBLE OF TEXAS

Facing page: Clara is surrounded by scurrying mice.
• BALLET ENSEMBLE OF TEXAS

scene with the three-headed Mouse King. The baby mice are precious, but the older ones are ferocious and wear frightening-looking masks.

The rehearsal demands can be heavy. In Michigan Classic Ballet or in Southeast Alabama Dance Company, for example, the mice are between eight and eleven years old, yet they must rehearse twenty-five to thirty hours over a fourteen-week period, prior to the first performance. "Our little ones must rehearse one hour a week for eight weeks," says Martha Goodman, a teacher at the Atlanta Ballet. "And they must continue their regular dance classes too." Does it seem like a lot of hours just to play the role of a little mouse? Each character, no matter how young, no matter how short their time on stage, must be fully rehearsed. A misplaced mouse could trip Clara or bump into one of the other characters, or even more frightening, the little mouse could be injured by quickly moving scenery.

Wendy Whelan in her first Nutcracker *with Louisville Ballet Company. Being a mouse is sometimes the beginning of a great career.*

Experienced artistic directors understand how much rehearsal time is enough for five to seven year olds, how much they need and how much they can endure before it stops being fun. "We limit rehearsal time to an hour or two each week for the small children," says Helen Starr, Associate Director of the Louisville Ballet. When they do rehearse, there is no time for anything but full attention to the task of character portrayal. "From the audition, the children understand we brook no nonsense, no talking, no bad behavior," Starr continues.

Once their child is cast, parents should expect to spend at least some part of every week right up to the opening performance at the studio or the

Boom!…boom!…boom! • BALLET ENSEMBLE OF TEXAS

One year, our production department loaded the cannon for the fight scene with flash powder as usual, but it had been left over from the previous year. Because it wasn't new, the powder had compressed, and the production department loaded an extra measure to fill the flash cavity. When it went off, there was a huge repeating boom . . . *boom!* . . . *boom!* . . . *boom!* so loud that children in the audience cried, the dust and smoke were dreadful and covered the wings and set. The little mouse, who was supposed to run on with the flag of surrender, looked at me wide-eyed. I gave her a pat, gently pushed her onto the stage with the traditional phrase "the show must go on," and as I looked up I realized that not one of the other mice had moved from their assigned places, they were so well rehearsed!

• MARY GEIGER, ARTISTIC
DIRECTOR OF MICHIGAN
CLASSICAL BALLET

theater. As the dancer grows from mouse to polichinelle to soldier, angel, attendant, flower fairy and then to soloist roles, the amount of time spent in rehearsal will grow, too. Professional dancers spend up to thirty hours per week in rehearsal as well as one-and-one-half to two hours a day in class. (Even when they aren't rehearsing or performing, professionals continue to spend many hours each week at the studio, taking class and working on variations.)

Helen Starr of the Louisville Ballet remembers a young boy looking at the stage for the first time and exclaiming "Wow! It's bigger than Sam's Club's Warehouse!"

After the audition, parents of the chosen dancers will be given a rehearsal and performance schedule and an informational handbook, along with parental consent forms to be signed, giving the company the right to use their child's photograph, providing emergency phone numbers, giving the identity of the person or persons who will be allowed to pick up their child from the theater, and agreeing to an understanding of the rehearsal demands on the child. A parent can look at the packet and know exactly what the time commitment will be right from the start."

Once the mice are chosen, rehearsals begin almost immediately. Initially, the little ones will be taught how to stay in line, how to stand quietly, learning who is in front of them and who is behind. Then they have to learn how to act like mice. Do they run or skip? Are they fast or slow? Do they stand about or move wildly? Eventually, the children begin to learn the steps of the mouse dance: slowly, one sequence at a time: three slides right . . . three slides left . . . stop! . . . jump and jump *plié* . . . over and over until each child knows the sequence thoroughly.

One day, a row of large wooden boxes on wheels appears in the studio, their doors open and costumes of every hue and color hanging on the racks inside, skirts and a few mouse tails spilling out onto the floor.

It is costume parade day.

All the company try on their costumes at one time to make sure that everyone has a costume and that they all fit properly and are complete. The costume parade in the studio could last an entire eight-hour workday.

At the next rehearsal, the director might say, "We're going to put yellow tape on the floor," pointing to several points around the studio. "Then we'll know how big the stage is going to be for your mouse dance." The dancers will walk around the taped area and get a feel for the dimensions, but as they do, they'll also notice another area outside the yellow zone marked with red tape.

"That's for the big mice," says the director who reminds them the big mice don't appear until the Mouse King comes face-to-face with the Nutcracker. The big mice are older children with more training, and their steps are more difficult, more intricate. When the battle begins, the big mice move into the yellow zone, as well, where they fight the soldiers.

The week before actual performances the entire company goes into the theater for rehearsals. Volunteers wait at the stage door to take the children to their dressing rooms. Parents are asked to leave, and the volunteer checks to make sure that the child's identification is registered correctly at the stage door. Each child has an identification card and number which gets them into the theater. During performances, they arrive one hour before their appearance on stage, go to their dressing rooms and get into costume. After they have performed, the children put on their street clothes again, give their identification card to the stage doorman and wait until a parent or guardian comes to pick them up, giving the stage doorman the matching identification number.

In most companies the younger children share a large conference or multipurpose room as a dressing room. Each cast of characters has a chaperone and at least one or two people to help them get dressed. With so many

It is costume parade day.
• VINELAND REGIONAL DANCE COMPANY

dancers entering and leaving the stage and milling about backstage, dressing room time is quite limited, so it's important everyone gets in and out quickly. Rarely is there room for parents behind the curtain. "In Atlanta the parents never come backstage," says Sharon Story. "We perform at an old theater that is quite cramped."

At the first stage rehearsal the children are taken to see the stage. The entire company will do a spacing rehearsal, where the little mice will use their colored tape once again. This rehearsal is followed by a technical rehearsal, which is not only for the dancers, but for the lighting and sound crew and all backstage personnel who move the scenery. It is at this crucial rehearsal that the children learn to get out of the way as the scenery moves around.

Excitement runs high: the big day of dress rehearsal arrives. The entire company must be at the theater at least one hour before to put on makeup, do their hair and warm up. Company professionals know they will be in their dressing rooms many hours during the four to six week run, so they make their dressing table areas as personal as they can, a fresh flower in a favorite vase, a good luck talisman hung on a mirror, or some special photos tucked inside the mirror . . . whatever they can do to make things homey.

Dressers and wardrobe crews carry armloads of colorful costumes to the appropriate dressing rooms or set them in the wings for fast change. Stagehands push and lift the scenery into its right place, often marked with tiny slivers of glow tape (called spikes) that can be seen on a darkened stage. Electricians make final lighting checks.

Soldiers in their dressing room
• PACIFIC NORTHWEST BALLET

After dress rehearsal, the director gives notes to the entire cast.

• VINELAND REGIONAL DANCE COMPANY

"Half-hour, ladies and gentlemen!" comes the call over the backstage PA system, and final preparations are made.

"Act One on stage!" comes the call twenty-five minutes later. Breathless scurrying, a final check in the mirror—makeup perfect?. . . . Costume complete?. . . . Hair smooth?. . . .

Chaperones accompany the young dancers onto the stage, making sure they are in the right places, then they slide away into the wings.

There is a hush as the first strains of the Tchaikovsky score fill the theater. The curtain slowly rises. . . .

Pacific Northwest Ballet mice are very specialized and danced by professional dancers.

Dress rehearsal has begun. It is just like a performance but without an audience. In most companies it will run without stops, but occasionally, especially with new productions, there will be stops to adjust the smoothness of a scene change, give the costumer last minute instructions or work out a spacing or tempo problem. Sometimes dress rehearsal can last into the late evening.

Just as each company has different needs so do they have different versions of the mouse dance. In the George Balanchine version (which is often considered the classic American *Nutcracker*) there is a "nurse" mouse who performs CPR and takes the pulse of Mouse King after he falls in combat with the Nutcracker. This mouse might wear a Red Cross armband and a nurse's cap, stuck between the huge pink ears, and may even carry a make-believe stethoscope. In the Louisville Ballet production, the mice are fought by soldiers who use huge feathers. "The mice are tickled to death," according to choreographer Alun Jones.

For each specialized mouse role the demands on the young dancer's skills increase. It's not uncommon for the dancer in the role of a leading mouse to have several years of *Nutcracker* experience, dancing as a little mouse, a rabbit, a party child, a polichinelle and perhaps even an Arabian Coffee attendant. How enveloping *Nutcracker* can become! One can begin as a five-year-old and remain in the production year after year, dancing a different and more demanding role each year until ready for one of the soloist challenges such as Coffee, Tea or even the Sugar Plum Fairy.

Chaperones watch quietly from the wings.
• BALLET ENSEMBLE OF TEXAS

March of the Toy Soldiers

A terrible battle begins—mice against soldiers, Mouse King against Nutcracker. Guns pop, cannons boom, swords clash. . . .

*I*n every Victorian toy chest little boys had toy soldiers, wooden ones, lead ones, tin ones, brightly painted in reds and blues and blacks and greens, smartly outfitted in the uniforms of their country's forces. They sent them into mock battle or arrayed them in parade or simply placed them around the room as talismans. It was the time of empires across the face of Europe, and children lived the adventures through their toy soldiers.

So too with the nutcracker doll, popular when E.T.A. Hoffman created his Victorian-era story. During Clara's dream early in Act One, as the Christmas tree grows, as the walls and furniture become bigger, so does her brother's toy box where his soldiers reside. The nutcracker toy soldier traditionally wears a shiny black peaked hat with red jacket and white trousers. But many ballet companies vary the costumes; at Pacific Northwest Ballet, for example, there are both cavalry and infantry soldiers in battle, each unit in different costume. Some companies place furry-busby Coldstream Guards hats on their soldiers, while others use the uniforms of Colonial Redcoats or the U.S. Confederacy. But no matter what the soldiers' costumes are, three particular items do not vary: all soldiers have carefully coiffed hair, stylized makeup and carry a prop.

From childhood, a female ballet dancer learns to wear her hair carefully slicked back in a bun or French twist because the look to be projected is always of a small and neat head, perched high and proudly on a long, slender neck. Even girls who play the parts of soldiers, where the hair is partly hidden in the hat, need to pay attention to their "look." At the ready must be a good supply of bobby pins, hairpins, combs, fabric-covered elastic bands, hairnets, hairspray, gels, shampoo, conditioner and a good hairbrush.

The most elaborate hairstyles in *Nutcracker* are those worn by the young and adult female guests in the Act One party scene. For women, a hairpiece

Putting hair up is a daily ritual, and it doesn't take long for a dancer to become adept at it no matter where she might be.

Facing page: Pacific Northwest Ballet has several different regiments of soldiers.

There are a number of styles the dancer can use for her bun, depending on her role or the vision of the choreographer:

The high bun—perched in the center of the head and also known as the "Balanchine" bun because he loved the graceful extension of neck it created. Female toy soldiers wear this style because it can be securely hidden under their hats.

The low bun—curled low on the nape of the neck. When combined with a curl on the cheek (either real or drawn with a black pencil) is used for more exotic roles such as the Spanish dancers (Chocolate) in Act Two.

The double bun—curled on either side of the head and named for the character of Princess Leah in "Star Wars."

The classical bun—the hair is parted in the middle and the two front pieces are dropped over the ears to a low bun. This style is used in some of the older ballets like *Giselle* or *Les Sylphides* but rarely used in *Nutcracker*.

styled with curls is the easiest way to attain the Victorian style. The dancer carefully curls her own hair to fall coyly around her face after attaching the curl-styled hairpiece to the back of her head. She sprays it all heavily so it will stay in place even when she's under warm lights and dancing vigorously.

In Victorian times, when little girls got ready for bed, their hair was twisted into tight strands and tied with rags of fabric. In the morning, the hair would be carefully brushed and produce perfect ringlets! It is not uncommon for young dancers to create ringlets and maintain them during the entire *Nutcracker* run, covering their heads with a scarf when attending school.

Makeup is another important aspect of the production. Some parents are concerned about how theatrical makeup will affect their child's delicate skin, but Boston makeup artist David Nicholas gently dismisses the issue. "Makeup is a staple in the theater," he says. "These days the products are much friendlier to the skin than they used to be." No more heavy greasepaint removed with layers of cold cream, no more thick foundation smears, no more wet liner pencils that bleed onto the fingers. He, along with many directors and other professional makeup artists, advises young dancers to have their own makeup kit that can last through many seasons of *Nutcracker*. Even when young dancers are performing in companies that use a professional makeup artist, it's important to have one's own sponges and brushes. The key is to use some foundation, because, as Nicholas says, "the most important makeup lesson a young dancer should learn is the care of her skin." And a good foundation, he insists, is where it begins.

Victorian ringlets on party children • OLYMPIC BALLET THEATRE

Spanish dancers wear a low bun.
• THE NEW YORK CITY BALLET

A bow attached to a mid-bun
• VINELAND REGIONAL DANCE COMPANY

The Olympic Ballet has a unique approach to the hair-styles of young dancers. Once the female party children have been chosen, parents are given an appointment to have a special hairstyle designed for their child. The parents are shown how to achieve the style and expected to practice. A month or so later, they are brought into the studio and examined to see if the hair will hold. "They rarely pass the first time," laughs Artistic Director Helen Wilkins, "so we ask them to practice more. By the time they have it right the children's hair will stay put throughout the most rigorous performance!"

Makeup serves a dual purpose: it highlights the dancers' features and it provides a uniform look. Bright theater lights tend to wash out and blur a dancer's features. From the back of the orchestra seats or high in the balcony, the audience would not see a dancer's lovely brown eyes or rosebud lips, so they must be exaggerated and intensified by makeup. It takes a makeup artist who understands lighting and the size of the theater to design specific makeup that will be uniform for dancers in similar roles. For example, a huge theater such as Boston's Wang Centre or New York's Metropolitan Opera House with its soaring golden balconies will require stronger and bolder makeup for dancers than a performance in a school auditorium.

How is makeup applied? First, a foundation (a liquid) is used, serving as canvas for the makeup design. In the past, foundations used greasepaint, but now crayon sticks that are not so shiny are preferred. Pancake (powder used with a damp sponge) can also be used, as it is easy to apply and stays in place well. Once the foundation is applied, the canvas is ready to paint. First are the cheeks. They should be accentuated with blush which comes in a cream or powder. Either works well. Next, the eyebrows should be shaped and darkened, and to increase the space between the eye and darkened brow, a pale pink or white shadow can be used. The color of eye shadow should compliment the costume colors.

Exaggeration of the eye is probably the most important single makeup technique a ballet dancer will acquire. With a dark pencil or liquid eyeliner, the line of the lashes is extended straight out, both above and below the eye, taking care that the lines are parallel. Then, a white cream shadow is applied

between these lines to bolster the illusion of immense eye size. Finally, a small red dot is placed at the inner edge of the eye.

For older dancers, false eyelashes are glued with a thin line of spirit glue on the eyelid, above and below the eye. The newest fake eyelashes can be purchased with glitter, but these are only used with magical *Nutcracker* characters like fairies and angels. Glitter, however, is used elsewhere in *Nutcracker,* often sprinkled on cheeks and around eyes by young dancers to enhance their look, and scattered over shoulders and torsos in the *Waltz of the Flowers* and the *Dewdrop* variations.

Ken Duncan, ballet master, applies Act One "doll" makeup.

• BALLET ENSEMBLE OF TEXAS

Polichinelles, in makeup, awaiting their cue.

Soldiers do not wear glitter! . . . just a careful coating of dark mascara on the eyelashes.

Artistic directors have definite ideas on lipstick color for most *Nutcracker* characters, but when it comes to the soldiers, the color should match the bright red circles that are applied to their cheeks, either by makeup or glued fabric spots. At the Olympic Ballet, the clowns and soldiers have their makeup applied by an assembly line of volunteers. The first volunteer applies the white or skin tone foundation, the next, the blush, and then the eyes, and so on until the makeup is uniformly applied to all the dancers.

At last, the battalion of soldiers is ready to go into battle. They make their line and pick up their guns, and now each one is holding a *prop*. A prop (short for property) is an object that appears on stage but isn't scenery. "It's not a costume or a hat," says Sharon Foley of the Royal Shakespeare Company property shop. "Props are moved on and off stage." And they add to the telling of the story.

There are a great many props in *Nutcracker,* especially in Act One. In the opening party scene, gifts, dancing shoes, dolls, musical instruments, whistles, trays of drinks and food, fans and roses are just a few of the necessary props. In the fight scene between the soldiers, the mice and Mouse King, there are swords, scimitars, guns, a drum, a bugle, a stretcher (for the fallen Mouse King), a stethoscope, cannon ammunition (often large chunks of "cheese" to be shot at the mice), a shoe (for Clara to throw at the Mouse King) and assorted other special variations such as Louisville Ballet's feathers to tickle the mice into submission!

Large companies have a prop man, an individual assigned to deal, specifically, with all props. He or she is responsible to see that every item is in its place at the beginning of each performance so dancers can pick up their props as they go on stage. The prop man is in charge of the prop tables that are located on either side of the stage. These are usually covered with white paper or white cloth, and each prop's shape is outlined in ink so the dancers, volunteers and backstage crew know what goes where.

So many props.
• PACIFIC NORTHWEST BALLET

Quietly, the soldiers are handed their guns as they arrive in the stage area. They line up behind their guard (toy) box, and they have to be absolutely silent because Clara is onstage alone and the music is soft as the mice creep out from under the tree. No call to arms here: the soldiers must know the music and be ready for their cue.

"Musically, the soldiers are the hardest to rehearse," says Louisville Ballet's Helen Starr, "the music is difficult to count." But well-rehearsed soldiers will know the cue, and on stage they march in perfect formation, tallest soldiers in back, led by a drumming or bugling bunny. They stand at attention as the

Nutcracker, their leader, confronts the three-headed Mouse King. Everyone is frozen for an instant. . . .

And then chaos erupts! The battle is on!

Every soldier must know his or her exact place and movement. A cannon-firing soldier knows the cannon is wheeled on stage and stopped at exactly the same spot, marked by a spike (a piece of silver tape) at every performance. The soldier must always leave the stage the same way, downstage, where soldier Susie is fighting mouse Margaret, but upstage of Clara's bed. . . .

The choreography for the fight scene is very specific. If a mouse chooses the wrong soldier to carry off stage, the cannon may lose its triggerman. If a soldier bumps the Mouse King out of position, there may be no target for Clara's shoe. Things are happening rapidly and at a high pitch. Often, the chaos of the fight scene is danced while stage lights are low and strobe lights are flashing.

In real life, soldiers speak of "the fog of war." In the *Nutcracker* fight scene, the audience gets a momentary glimpse of it through the fog of smoke created by the cannon fire. For *Nutcracker* soldiers, "controlled chaos" is the more operative phrase.

Bunnies, Bears and Prickly Pears

Crash! Boom! Out of one of the toy boxes march a squad of toy soldiers, led by a rabbit (or sometimes a brown bear) and like the mice they are as tall as Clara. . . .

*M*ore than five hundred dance companies—many doing their own specialized version— perform *Nutcracker* somewhere in America each Christmas season.

The most acclaimed and best known is the Balanchine version premiered by New York City Ballet in 1954 and danced annually at New York's Lincoln Center. It sets the standard for traditional productions. But it is a fragile standard, because so many other companies and choreographers have taken the story, along with Tchaikovsky's music, and adapted it. For example, in 2002, Matthew Bourne, a contemporary ballet choreographer, premiered his version at Saddlers Wells Theatre in London. It opens with a woebegone Clara in Dr. Dross's Orphanage before moving through an ice-filled extravaganza in Sweetieland and the high energy explosion of a Busby Berkeley musical.

In the Balanchine production, the toy soldiers are led into battle against the mice by a white, drum-beating bunny. Boston Ballet has a bunny, as well. It's not a drum-beating bunny; this one blows a bugle, and he (or she) has an added responsibility: the bunny has to scoop up and save the tiniest mouse when the mouse is in danger.

In 1947 William and Lew Christensen produced the first American *Nutcracker* for the San Francisco (California) Ballet. The production included a dancing bear as one of Dr. Drosselmeyer's mechanical toys (in addition to the beautiful ballerina and multicolored harlequin). When Lew Christensen took the production to Ballet West (Utah) some years later, the dancing bear went along. Bruce Marks, a principal dancer with Ballet West and subsequently its artistic director, continued to use the dancing bear, and, years later, when he took the position as Boston Ballet's artistic director, the dancing bear came with him.

Facing page: Dancers skate in an icy Sweetieland in Matthew Bourne's Nutcracker!
• NEW ADVENTURES COMPANY

Robert Dekkers, now a dancer with Ballet Arizona in Tucson, remembers being that bunny in his first *Nutcracker* at the Atlanta Ballet under artistic director Robert Barnett, a former New York City Ballet dancer. "I had to run around the stage and pull the Mouse King's tail. That was the best part. I think I decided right there I wanted to be a performer."

Jamie Wolf, now a dancer with New York City Ballet, started her career as a bunny.

Campbell Baird's dancing bear.
• OREGON BALLET THEATRE

The year Marks arrived at Boston Ballet, the famed department store, Filene's, offered a "Filene's Bear" for Christmas sale. Aha! thought the Ballet development people, let's have our designer dress the Boston Ballet bear like the Filene Bear. Think of the free advertising, maybe even some funding! The connection was made, and while Filene's Bear may still be around, we *know* Boston Ballet's *Nutcracker* bear continues to dance each year.

The Pacific Northwest Ballet had been doing the Christensen *Nutcracker* for years when coartistic directors Francia Russell and her husband Kent Stowell thought it was time for the company to have its own special production. Because their two small boys loved everything by the artist Maurice Sendak, they thought "why not ask him?" Although Sendak designed for the opera, he had not worked on a ballet production. When he saw how dedicated the dancers were to achieving perfection in their work, he agreed to do the job.

Sendak's unusual touch showed clearly. The E.T.A. Hoffman story remained, but now there is a whip-wielding pasha who acts as master of ceremonies throughout Act Two, and an exquisite bird in a gilded cage brings life and beauty to the Arabian music. The children of Mother Ginger dance in a miniature pastoral scene instead of around Mother Ginger. Of course, the Sugar Plum Fairy remains.

When artistic director Linda Walker of the Tucson (Arizona) Regional Ballet was planning a new *Nutcracker* some years ago, she wanted to use a special motif, something that would mirror the culture and the traditions of Arizona and the Southwest. The storyline begins this way: Tio (Uncle) Diego

(Drosselmeyer), a magical guest at a Christmas party, brings three life-size dolls to entertain: a gambler, a gunslinger and a hurdy-gurdy girl. At the party, given by the parents of Maria and Pepito, Maria receives a toy nutcracker from her Tio which is dressed as a U.S. Cavalry general. Her jealous brother, Pepito, snatches it and breaks the toy.

When Maria comes downstairs in the middle of the night, she is greeted, not by mice, but by a coyote! The Christmas tree begins to grow (as it always does), the clock strikes twelve, the Cavalry General Nutcracker appears, sword

In the Matthew Bourne version, there are non-traditional and imaginative costumes, scenery and choreography.

• NEW ADVENTURES COMPANY

in hand, to battle the Coyote King, and story moves in traditional steps through a snow scene atop local peak, Mount Lemmon. At a Desert Dream they are welcomed by a Native American princess, prairie children and the Prickly Pear Fairy (Sugar Plum) and her Caballero! The traditional delicacies are here, though not as we would expect: there are chili peppers, rattlesnakes, tumbleweeds and desert flowers.

The story is so fanciful, so adaptable, that the setting of the Stahlbaum family is changeable, too. Matthew Bourne set his *Nutcracker!* in a bleak Dickensian orphanage with Clara as a drab, sad character. Mark Morris, America's maverick choreographer, set his 1950s-era opening scene of *The Hard Nut* in stark suburbia. Clara and Fritz are self-indulgent and bratty, their mother a cocktail-drinking show-off who dances in high heels while welcoming a group of characters in shiny plastic, bell bottoms and mini skirts to the party. In the finale, Clara and her brother are curled up watching televison!

Each year the Greensboro (North Carolina) Ballet does a single *Nutcracker* spoof performance during its regular *Nutcracker* season. In the snow scene, the *corps de ballet* starts out in traditional pristine costumes, but each time a dancer leaves the stage, she returns with hat, mittens, scarf and hockey stick until the scene ends with a hockey battle! And Clara? She and her Prince (named Elvis) travel to Las Vegas and meet a *corps* of green-clad male flowers in long green underwear with "tutu" emblazoned on their heads. Heidi Strohl, former company member, recalls that the opening party scene guests included Barbie and Ken, Scarlett and Rhett, Laverne and Shirley and Lucy and Desi. "I think it made our regular performances better because we were all really relaxed after making complete fools of ourselves!"

Snow and Magic

"Come with me," the Prince urges, "I'll show you the wonders of my kingdom." She takes his hand, and he guides her to the window, leading her out to an enchanted snow forest. . . .

As Clara and her Prince enter the Enchanted Forest, they come upon the dazzling spectacle of falling snow, heralded by the Snow Queen and her Cavalier. It is a turning point in the *Nutcracker* story, as Clara passes from reality to the land of fantasy. How better to project such a transformation than with a shimmering, elegant curtain of snow through which they must glide!

A corps of snowflakes.
• THE NEW YORK CITY BALLET

On stage, the falling snow offers an illusion that enraptures both adults and children. The theater transports the audience to a place of magic where anything is possible, even a fresh snowfall.

The *Nutcracker* story offers one marvelous bit of magic after another, captivating even George Balanchine, who was known for the simplicity of the staging of his ballets. Often, he used a clear, blank *cyclorama* (a screen at the rear of the stage) and simple chiffon skirts for his costumes, no matter how

Facing page: The Prince guides Clara on a magical journey.
• BALLET ENSEMBLE OF TEXAS

complex the choreography or story were. Not so with his *Nutcracker.* It is exquisitely lush, especially the snow scene, where he set towering white trees, a soaring sleigh and a *corps de ballet* of sixteen dancers, each holding wands of snow, delicately gliding through a curtain of falling snow.

For young dancers, being cast as a snowflake is an indication that a certain level of childhood ballet skill has been achieved, and more demanding parts will follow. The dancing in the snow scene is often on pointe, and the choreography is more intricate than that of the children's dances in the party scene or the mouse and soldier fight scene. The dancers must also learn to cope with falling snow, which can be slippery; it can get in their hair and inside their costumes. In many American *Nutcracker* productions the snow falls across the entire stage. At the Bolshoi theater in Moscow, the snow falls at stage rear, piling up in one location so the dancers can seem to be cavorting in the snow but they don't have to be afraid of slipping.

San Francisco Ballet uses approximately one hundred pounds of flame-proofed recycled paper snow at each performance. Other companies sweep up the snow to be used again. This approach can be dangerous as foreign objects might find their way into snow bags, large muslin containers hung high above the stage. The containers have a number of two-inch wide slits, three or four inches apart, and when shaken, out comes all the snow! New York City Ballet, which reuses its snow, has special roller magnets that filter the snow for hair pins and bits of other metal, after it has landed on stage and been swept up for reuse.

Sometimes, snowballs are carried.
• VINELAND REGIONAL DANCE COMPANY

Anything is possible, even
a fresh snowfall.
• BALLET ENSEMBLE OF TEXAS

Mary Geiger of Michigan Classic Ballet recalls a moment when the magic went awry. "Our snow bag dumped all one hundred pounds of the snow at once, and of course it was when the dancers were in a *cambré* (bending backwards movement). The dancers were unable to get out of the way, and suddenly the stage resembled a blizzard scene with everyone snow-covered."

Snowflakes, dancing on pointe • PACIFIC NORTHWEST BALLET

The magic of the performance starts long before the snow scene. In the first moments of Act One, as Clara and Fritz peek through the living room door at their parents preparing for arriving guests, they seem to be standing in front of a solid wall. As the lights come up in the parlor, the wall disappears, and the audience is treated to a full view of what Clara and Fritz see—their parents preparing for their guests!

How is it done? The set or *drop* that is the wall and door is painted on a gauze fabric known as a *scrim*. This fabric can be seen through when lit from the back, but otherwise appears impenetrable. So, the lights dim in the hallway where Clara and Fritz stand and grow bright in the parlor where the Stahlbaums prepare for the party. The scrim is lit from the back, and suddenly there's no wall. The audience sees the parents bustle about, even though a moment before, Clara and Fritz were looking through a door in a seemingly solid wall.

No one who has ever seen *The Nutcracker* can forget the magical growing Christmas tree. At New York City Ballet, the tree is eighteen feet high during the opening party, but as Clara watches it grow, it becomes forty-one feet high by the time the snow scenery flies in (at the same time, the doll's bed, the walls, the fireplace, the paintings and the grandfather clock also grow!).

There are as many ways to make the tree grow as there are set designers. Some trees grow from a trap door onstage, some with pulley systems worked from backstage. Some trees are hung on the theater grid, which is a pipe flown high above the stage. Most artistic directors are loath to be too specific about how their particular system might work. "Too much information breaks the magic," they say, and they add, "All directors need to keep *some* secrets!"

The magic of *Nutcracker* abounds: the flash of lightning as Drosselmeyer enters…the muzzle flash of the cannon as the soldiers fight the mice. It is done with flash pots, steel cylinders mounted on electric boxes that detonate.

The tree starts at ten feet . . .
• BALLET ENSEMBLE OF TEXAS

. . . and grows and grows and grows!
• BALLET ENSEMBLE OF TEXAS

How does the doll's bed move? "It's always the most asked question when people come on a backstage tour," says Perry Silvey, New York City Ballet Production Manager. "I ask the kids how they think it's done, and my favorite answer came from a small boy, who said, 'I know how it's done . . . there's a man under the stage with a big magnet just walking around!'"

Clara on the magic moving life-size doll bed.
• NEW JERSEY BALLET

How does Clara's bed move during the transition scene in Act One of the New York City Ballet's *Nutcracker?* Thirty years ago there was a "bed boy," a ballet student under the bed, crawling around the stage, moving the bed that was on wheels. It is done the same way today.

One of the most exciting moments for Clara and her Prince is the ride high above the stage in the magic sleigh. In the San Francisco Ballet, the children hover twenty-two feet above the stage, and in the New York City Ballet they travel three-quarters of the way across the stage at a height of eighteen feet before the curtain descends on Act One. "Each cast has two rehearsals in the sleigh, and they love it, "says Perry Silvey.

Not all companies have angels floating through drifting clouds, but those that do know well the magic of dry ice and the extraordinary amounts needed to make its effects fill the stage. According to Brad Fields of American Ballet Theatre, to cover the stage at New York's Metropolitan Opera House it requires four separate ice machines with fifty pounds of dry ice in each to make those drifting clouds—equaling two hundred pounds of dry ice for a single stage effect so the magic will prevail! "It depends on the day, the humidity and the temperature of the heating and cooling systems," he says, noting there are continual adjustments to oversee. "But it always gives me a thrill to watch the clouds gently move and drift with the dancers."

Not every production can afford the mechanical devices to make all that magic happen. When money is scarce, it takes a bit of ingenuity and determination to use what *is* available. When Vermont Ballet Theatre produced its

A snow scene created with lights • VERMONT BALLET THEATRE

1991 *Nutcracker* at the Barre Opera House in Montpelier, there were almost
no sets. The company was small and on a limited budget. There was no living
room set for the party scene, no snow, no fog . . . it was done with lights.
From the opening scene and the towering parlor window, draped with heavy
curtains, the snow scene's fairy castle with winter white fir trees and soft blue
clouds dropping huge snowflakes, to the arrival of angels on pink clouds: all

of these were created by the use of *gobos*. These are small metal templates that are slipped in between the lamp (or bulb) and the lens of an ellipsoidal lighting instrument that can be focused onto the cyclorama.

In the Hartford (Connecticut) Ballet's *Nutcracker,* choreographed and produced by Michael Uthoff in the 1980s and 1990s, there is no snow! He used a revolving mirror ball, immersing not only the stage but the entire theater in falling images.

The sheer beauty of the snow scene is one of the most memorable in all of classical ballet. At the ballet's premiere in 1892, many critics weren't sure what to call the overall performance because it contained so much more than what they were used to seeing as ballet. But one critic, possessed by the memory of the falling snow, the fantasy and the beauty of scene after scene used a single word for it all. A "spectacle," he called it. And so it is.

Act Two

Music and Angels

"Mine is the Kingdom of Sweets,"
says the Prince, "but first, we must fly
past the angels. . . ."

The curtain sweeps up to the swelling sounds of harp and violin as Act Two opens on the Kingdom of Sweets. Clara and her Prince are about to meet the Sugar Plum Fairy and her court of dancing delicacies.

When the Ballet Russe de Monte Carlo toured America in the 1940s, the company danced only Act Two, a perfect vehicle for its array of stars like Alexandra Danilova, Alicia Markova, Andre Eglevsky and David Lichine. Although the company had lavish sets and costumes, the set for Act Two was relatively simple to tour, and the performance became known as *The Nutcracker Suite,* because it embraced a series of dances rather than a complete story. It is here in this act that dancers show off their technique and talents.

As the music swells, the stage swirls with drifting clouds, softly lit with pink light. A *corps de ballet* of shimmering angels glides on, halos and wings swaying gently, wispy forms, half-distinct. The dancer who leads the angels must be among the most musical of the group. Size and leadership qualities are important but musicality, or the ability to recognize tempo and stay with the music, is essential for any dancer cast to lead a group of other dancers and who aspires to a professional career.

The *Nutcracker* score is divided into an overture and fifteen sections. In the first scene of Act One the music helps to maintain the structure of the story: the march is for the children, the entrance of Dr. Drosselmeyer is heralded by the violas and tenor trombone and the traditional Victorian Grossvater's (Grandfather's) Dance brings the party to an end. As the party-goers leave, a calm melody sends them on their way.

The music turns suspenseful as Clara creeps down the stairs, the clock striking midnight and mice scurrying across the stage. Violins and harps begin their soaring melody as the tree begins to grow. All the action is there in the

Facing page: Angels come in all sizes.
• BALLET ENSEMBLE OF TEXAS

"I remember when I was an angel. I'd never heard the music before and my teacher made me the lead angel. It was so hard to count at first, even though I had sung when I was younger. But the teacher was adamant that I was going to lead so I just had to learn."

• JESSIE FRY, NOW A DANCER WITH MARYLAND BALLET THEATRE.

Peter Ilyitch Tchaikovsky

"*Nutcracker* is Tchaikovsky's best score," says Boston Ballet's music librarian, Arthur Leeth. "It's exquisite programmatic music. Unfortunately, we tend to grow immune to its effects because we hear it so often in less-exquisite surroundings such as television commercials, elevators and shopping malls. We need to focus on the richness of the music."

music: a shot is fired, a drum roll calls the soldiers to the fight scene, and Clara's shoe hurtles through the air to strike the Mouse King. Through his music, Tchaikovsky saw the story clearly.

As they go into the Land of Snow, the music underscores the transition with a *pas de deux* for Clara and her Prince to signify the journey, and the same music tells the stagehands to begin the falling snow. In the Act One finale, a choir of children's voices rings out

As Act Two opens, Clara and her Prince approach the Kingdom of Sweets. Tchaikovsky had difficulty, at the beginning, expressing exactly what he wished to convey. He admitted to his brother, "I am groping in the dark; finding it impossible to express musically the Sugar Plum Kingdom." Eventually, he overcame the problems with glorious results: in the judgment of many, the divertissements in Act Two contain the most familiar and beloved of all his ballet music. The music that supports the entrance of the angels in the opening of Act Two "is so crystalline and pure," says Arthur Leeth, Boston Ballet's music librarian. "The way he weaves all the underlying parts of the orchestra together is simply incredible." As the angels glide through soft pink clouds, with harps, lyres and candles aloft, the music invokes ethereal grace, and the audience is transported. The crucial role played by angels in the overall production presents a heavenly world far removed from everyday reality.

The angels are actually highly trained young dancers who are in class as much as two hours *each* day, along with the regular weekly rehearsals for their roles. Somehow, they also carry full high school academic loads. In some companies the angels dance on pointe, but at Boston Ballet, among others, the angels do *not* dance on pointe in order to achieve a smoother, quieter, more delicate quality.

In the production choreographed by Rudolf Nureyev for the Royal Swedish Ballet and now danced by Britain's Royal Ballet Company, Clara dances a *pas de deux* with her prince until he leaves her alone on stage, no angels to guide her, no clouds to carry her along, and she is attacked by huge bats! The bats turn into parents and other adults from the opening party scene and the story continues traditionally. Yet the music makes this version, and every other version, believable, which attests to the underlying power of Tchaikovsky's genius.

When the Sugar Plum Fairy enters, a new sound is introduced, something between a tinkle and a soft chord, almost otherworldly. It is the sound of a *celesta* (also called a *celeste*), a piano-like instrument whose hammers strike steel plates providing an ethereal sound. It plays the music of the Sugar Plum Fairy *only,* and it is her special instrument. *Nutcracker* is one of the few ballets in which one instrument plays for a specific character. In Act Two, the celesta accompanies Sugar Plum whenever she is on stage.

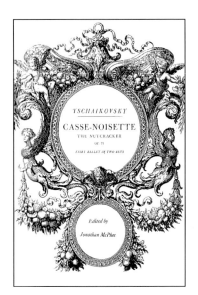

The original Russian score.

"We actually use young dancers who play soldiers and Bonbons to sing the Act One finale," says Boston Ballet's Arthur Leeth. "Our casts are so large, anyway, that an additional thirty or forty bodies backstage would sorely tax our facilities."

"It's music you can see and feel, which makes it easy for us to remember and to commit to our muscle memory," says Jessie Fry, now a principle with Maryland Ballet Theatre, who has been dancing to Tchaikovsky's music since she was seven. "When I as an angel, I decided I really wanted to be Clara, so I learned her part from the back of the studio. Every night when I went home, all I would do was dance Clara. I think I became Clara at home! But I loved being an angel. We all felt like we were floating."

Angels of Vermont Ballet Theatre.

In the Balanchine and in the Pacific Northwest Ballet versions, the Sugar Plum Fairy dances her famous variation when she first appears, giving the audience a better awareness of the celesta. In other *Nutcrackers,* her variation is danced as part of the *grand pas de deux* at the end of Act Two.

Although Tchaikovsky's music and ballet are bonded seamlessly, *Nutcracker* was one of only three ballets he composed (*Swan Lake* and *The Sleeping Beauty* are the other two). But many of his other works have been

The celesta score

It is said that Tchaikovsky heard the celesta in Paris when on tour in 1890, and was so enchanted that he composed the Sugar Plum Fairy's music specifically for the instrument. He worked quickly, determined to incorporate the celesta for the December 1892 premiere of his *Nutcracker*.

adapted to ballet choreography, such as Balanchine's exquisite *Serenade* to *Serenade for String Orchestra,* Gerald Arpino's *Reflections* set to *Variations on a Rococo Theme* and Sir Kenneth Macmillan's *Anastasia,* which used Tchaikovsky's First and Third Symphonies. Isadora Duncan danced to his Sixth Symphony *(Symphony Pathetique).*

The Sugar Plum Fairy and Other Delicacies

"My loyal subjects will dance for you," the Sugar Plum Fairy says as she leads them to a pair of golden thrones and royally claps her hands. . . .

*I*n traditional Act Two versions, Clara and her Prince are welcomed to the Kingdom of Sweets and meet the legendary Sugar Plum Fairy, ballet's most famous character.

As Queen of the Kingdom and gracious hostess, she offers them an array of dancing delectables: Chocolate, Tea, Coffee, Bonbons, Marzipan (by tradition represented by the Shepherdess Mirlitons) and Ginger, all principal roles in Act Two. Directors fill these roles with dancers with a certain "look:" dark haired dancers for Chocolate, the Spanish variation; tiny, precise dancers for Tea, the Chinese variation; long, slender dancers for Coffee, the sensuous Arabian variation.

"How did you get to my Kingdom of Sweets?" Sugar Plum asks Clara and the Prince. In a thirty-one bar section of the music the young Nutcracker Prince tells her about Clara having saved his life in the battle with the Mouse King and how her love and bravery has broken the spell which had kept him a wooden toy. "You must be rewarded," she responds, and she commands the delicacies of her kingdom to perform.

Because sweets and candy are part of a modern child's daily life, it's hard to imagine that in the nineteenth century, when *Nutcracker* first appeared, sugar and candy were quite difficult to attain in Europe. Only affluent families could afford them, and they were limited to special occasions. It is not surprising, therefore, that there is a special significance for each character in the Kingdom of Sweets.

In the cornucopia of Act Two variations, there is a shared uniformity among *Nutcracker* productions, whether contemporary or traditional. In Mark Morris's *The Hard Nut,* the Nutcracker Prince travels the world to see variations in Spain, China and Russia; in Matthew Bourne's 2002 restaged *Nutcracker!* variations include dancers performing as Licorice, Marshmallows,

Wendy Whelan as Sugar Plum Fairy.
• THE NEW YORK CITY BALLET

Facing page: Sugar Plum Fairy and her Cavalier perform the grand pas de deux as Clara and her Prince watch from their candy-cane thrones.
• NEW JERSEY BALLET

Playful Tea from China
• OLYMPIC BALLET THEATRE

The New York City Ballet's Joyful Tea

King Sherbet and Queen Candy. In *Nutcrackers* such as George Balanchine's 1950s version, there are Coffee, Tea and Candy Cane variations.

Performing in the variations requires solid ballet skills, and it is usually the most advanced company dancers who do them, working with *guest artists* who will dance the premier roles of Sugar Plum Fairy and her Cavalier. Generally, guest artists are principal dancers from a major ballet company, hired to perform for the *Nutcracker* season. They arrive shortly before the first performance in order to rehearse the Act Two opening with the entire company. If it is a dancer who will perform as Sugar Plum Fairy, she will often bring her regular partner, as well as her costume and her favorite choreography for the *grand pas de deux* variation and the coda.

Many guest artists and their partners travel with their own costumes, and sometimes they do so only after a hard lesson. Helen Starr, formerly a principal dancer with the Royal Ballet remembers such an occasion vividly. "I was dancing Snow Queen and went on stage in a company costume," she recalls. "At the first lift, I heard a low rip, and my partner whispered, 'It's ok,' and he held my costume closed. 'I'll adjust,' and he did. Thank goodness there was a dresser in the wings. She sewed me into the costume before my next entrance." After this, Starr *always* took her own costume along when she performed as a guest artist.

Imagine the awe and joy teenage ballet aspirants feel when a dancer such as Amanda McKerrow (or another principal dancer from a major company) performs with them, dances on the same stage on which they dance and in rare

Wendy Whelan as Arabian Coffee

A guest artist can offer company dancers a great deal more than professional role-filling. "I believe my presence (as a guest artist) is to teach through example," says American Ballet Theatre prima ballerina, Amanda McKerrow. "Working with young dancers helps me remember what it was like to dance as a teenager. It's important they understand that we're all sharing the same experience, and we're simply at different places on the road."

Russian Cossack dancers • BALLET ENSEMBLE OF TEXAS

Chocolate from Spain
• BALLET ENSEMBLE OF TEXAS

cases, even partners with them. "My teenage years were probably the happiest of my dancing years," adds McKerrow. As they watch rehearsals and performances, the young dancers come to understand the undeviating discipline professionals possess and how that carries them forward in a dance career.

"We often arrive to dance as a guest artist only a day or two before our performances," McKerrow says. "Of course, we're fully prepared before we get there. We've rehearsed the choreography, but we must learn to adapt to the different scenery, stage sizes, casts and productions." There is one thing she—and other guests artists—*can* rely on: the choreography for Sugar Plum Fairy tends to be traditional and follows the general outline set out in the original Ivanov/Petipa *Nutcracker* of 1892. If the music for the Sugar Plum *pas de deux* and resulting variations and coda are to be played with a full orchestra, the dancer must talk it through with the conductor to establish appropriate tempos. Both the dancer and the conductor understand that rarely will two dancers perform the Sugar Plum role exactly the same way. For example, there are some dancers who turn fast, requiring the music to speed up and keep up, while there are other dancers who will sweep on stage and hold a balance interminably, requiring the music to stretch itself in order to stay in time. Some dancers jump and fly quickly across the stage, while others soar slowly and gracefully. The accompaniment must accommodate them all.

Along with four walls, a roof and a stage, a theater is a repository of superstitions and a forum for proper etiquette. Having the guest artist's dressing room closest to the stage is a mark of respect and deference. Another is the attitude towards a guest's rehearsal. Young dancers must be aware of the concentration the artist requires to fit into the company, and if observing, they should never talk while the artist is rehearsing. Respect for the guest artist is traditional; two generations ago, it was common for younger dancers to curtsey as the guest artist passed by. Even today, in some European theaters such as the Paris Opera House, it's still practiced.

In Europe, superstitions abound. There's usually a brown toy bear on one of the dressing tables, and as dancers leave to go on stage, they rub it gently. Later, as the performance is to begin they will whisper *"merde"* to each other.

Amanda McKerrow's thoughts are echoed by Jessie Fry, now a principal dancer with Maryland Ballet Theatre and performing as Sugar Plum Fairy. "I remember how in awe I was when Diedre Carberry came to guest when I was with Delta Festival Ballet in New Orleans. I was on a high for days if she even spoke to me! I watched her rehearse for hours, and I know I learned so much more than technique. I learned what being a ballerina entails. I hope, as I continue to dance principal roles, that I can be that kind of inspiration to other young dancers."

Not every prima ballerina can execute thirty-two *fouettés* (fast, whipped turns) or a six o'clock *penché arabesque* (see photograph opposite), as the traditional Sugar Plum choreography requires. Neither the late Margot Fonteyn nor the early ballet icon, Anna Pavlova, was known for either. But their sheer charisma, their joy in performing their art, their intuitive sense of artistry carried them above their physical limits and made them memorable.

The Cavalier's costume must fit so that it moves with him. • BALLET ENSEMBLE OF TEXAS

Shortly before their entrance, dancers—guest artists, too—will consume yellow M&Ms—and they *must* be yellow! In a specific sense these traditions ensure a fine performance with no injury or performer embarrassment, but on a more general level, they establish a continuation with the past and a sense of belonging. "Ultimately, we're the products of our own superstitions," says a well-known artistic director. "We've turned them into rules for how we perform." She pauses, then adds: "There's nothing wrong with that!"

But Sugar Plum Fairy stands alone, and long-held ballet tradition supports the use of her own costume. Usually, it's in shades of darkest plum to palest pink, and she sparkles and shines at every entrance. And if she comes with her own partner, he will generally have his own costume, too, and it will blend with hers.

Sometimes, guest artists come in groups, instead of singly or as partners. At the Atlanta Ballet, Tea, or the Chinese variation, is performed by the Chinese Dance Company, a troupe of non-company-affiliated dancers. "It's a wonderful way to engage still another part of our community," says Sharon Story, who coordinates all student dancers in the Ballet's *Nutcracker.* Here, there are four separate casts of six dancers each, performing special choreography created by Artistic Director John McFall, and the dancers fit snugly into overall performance, even if they aren't members of the company or students in the company school.

When the late Alexander Bennett, founder of the Scottish-American Ballet, staged his *Nutcracker* for Twin Cities Ballet (Bloomington, Illinois) a few years ago, a troupe of Ukrainian dancers from Chicago came as guest artists and performed the exciting Russian variation in their own exquisitely embroidered costumes. The dancers restaged their usual routine to fit the more exuberant demands of Tchaikovsky's music, and Bennett remembered it as "a memorable performance, something *Nutcracker* audiences don't get to see very often."

In the ballet world, there are rarely enough strong male dancers. Many small companies find it difficult to fill all male roles in *Nutcracker,* so they often

The Sugar Plum Fairy and her Cavalier in an arabesque penché.
• VINELAND REGIONAL DANCE COMPANY

Guest artists are the essence of professionalism, and sometimes their skills will be called upon during the *Nutcracker* experience. "I was dancing Sugar Plum one season," recalls Helen Starr. "I went on to greet Clara and her Prince in the opening of Act Two, but I could see there was a commotion backstage. When I came off, I was told that the person who was to perform Mother Ginger had not turned up, and it was getting close to his cue. Well," she laughs, "there was only one thing to do!" She peeled off her Sugar Plum tutu, donned the Mother Ginger wig and dress and with fan in hand was lifted to her partner's shoulder and carried on stage. "The children under the skirt were quietly giggling because their ballerina was playing a man, playing a woman! Ten minutes later I was back in my tutu dancing the Sugar Plum *pas de deux!*"

import male dancers. There are several avenues to search. Primary sources are professional booking agents who represent dancers, and many can be found through listings in the major dance magazines or by contacting the public relations departments of major ballet companies. Directors also share with one another knowledge of, and experiences with, guest artists, and woe to unreliable or attitudinal artists because their reputations will precede them everywhere.

When hiring a guest artist for a major *Nutcracker* role through a booking agent, the key is planning. The moment the current season ends, the director must begin negotiating with the artist or his or her agent for *next* season. "It's like producing Thanksgiving dinner," says New York City agent Mark Kappel. "You don't start planning the party on Thanksgiving Day. You plan ahead! You must know your budget, the dates of your performances and how many there will be. The sooner the contract is ready to be offered, the more likely the best choice will be available, especially with male dancers."

Ultimately, the *Nutcracker* guest artist serves a dual role: first, he or she performs for the duration of the season; but second, he or she is a role model for the young dancers in the company. The latter role is as satisfying as the former. "I loved to guest," says retired dancer Teresina Goheen whose career took her to the Tulsa Ballet Theatre (Oklahoma), Dayton Ballet (Ohio) and principal roles with Fort Wayne Ballet (Indiana). "You have such a responsibility to the younger dancers. You teach them by your actions the ethic of hard work and respect for their directors, rehearsal teachers, costumers and crew. Most importantly, though, you teach them their responsibility to their art!

Amanda McKerrow as Sugar Plum Fairy. A guest artist sets an example for the younger dancers.

Mother Ginger And Her Children

"Look!" points the Prince, and huge woman, as tall as a cherry tree, lumbers on stage, carrying a plumed fan. . . .

A *polichinelle* is a character originally created in the *Commedia dell'arte,* the sixteenth century Italian street theater. That character, *Puncinella,* a pot-bellied, scheming, bragging rascal, became *Polichinelle* as the art form spread across France and developed into a highly successful puppet and marionette show. As created by the Parisian Jean Brioche, Polichinelle was a humpback with an enormous hooked nose and sported floppy white clothes and a pointed hat. Asked why he created Polichinelle, Brioche replied, "For the pleasure of the children of France!" That grotesque character has developed today into *Nutcracker's* outsized Mother Ginger.

Backstage, Mother Ginger develops this way: there is a lonely hook with only a very large hoop skirt hanging from it. It seems forgotten until the call comes:

"Stand by, Ginger skirt."

"Stand by, Mother Ginger!"

"Stand by, kids."

"Go skirt! . . ." On the command, the hoop contraption floats gracefully over a man wearing pantaloons that cover a pair of stilts. He towers over anyone else. (At the New York City Ballet, the stilts are eighteen inches tall!)

"Heads!" the call that every dancer must learn, the warning that something is flying down from above. Mother Ginger's skirt can weigh between thirty and fifty pounds!

"Skirt in!" and the huge skirt settles around the man now sporting a bright orange wig and showing exaggerated cupid bow lips and fluttering eyelashes.

"Go kids!" comes the next command. The stage door opens and a dozen little children, the polichinelles, scuttle under the skirt. They are often

The huge skirt must be held up high in the air backstage.
• BALLET ENSEMBLE OF TEXAS.

Facing page: The polichinelles burst forth from under the skirt to dance.
• OLYMPIC BALLET THEATRE

"I always wanted to be a polichinelle," says Heidi Strohl of Northern Ballet Theatre, "but I was too tall. It always looked like so much fun and those kids seemed to be such special friends by the end of *Nutcracker!*"

A pasha, the master of ceremonies.
• PACIFIC NORTHWEST BALLET

"You had to be pretty small to be a polichinelle, or a Gingerette as they are called in Arizona's Ballet Etudes," remembers Jessie Phettaplace. "Some of the dancers could also do gymnastic tricks. I remember one girl had to do a back flip before she ran back under the skirt. One night she flipped right into the frame of the skirt—which was heavy metal. Fortunately she didn't get hurt but it took a bit of clever improvisation to untangle her."

dressed in the traditional white costume with long, floppy arms and pointed hats, though other variations resembled another *Commedia dell'arte* character, *Pierrot,* who appeared in two-color checkered clown costume, tight skull cap and a sequined tear glistening on one cheek.

"Stand by, lights."

"Stand by, music."

A pause, then . . . "go lights . . . go music . . . go Mother! . . ."

The production crew, the stage manager, the lighting technicians, the orchestra, the stagehands and the prop men all are part of the backstage family, working together to make magic. It is a hierarchy with a set of rules and responsibilities and clearly defined manners. They know the physical safety of the cast depends on them, and they understand how a wrong call, a forgotten warning, a carelessly hung light can cause injury, even disaster! It is a big family, and sometimes, in the largest theaters, as many as one hundred sixty people can be working backstage.

A prop man hands the huge "woman" a feather fan to flutter, the lights and music rise together, and the oversized travesty called Mother Ginger sidles onstage with a dozen tiny polichenelles under her skirt ready to burst forth and dance.

The audience responds with laughter and applause, the magic of *Nutcracker* once more in evidence. It should be noted not every production of *Nutcracker* contains the classic Mother Ginger and her polichinelles. At Oregon Ballet Theatre, former Artistic Director James Canfield made Mother Ginger a chef, and the polichinelles Bonbons who arrive on stage in a huge ice cream sundae dish. At Pacific Northwest Ballet the polichinelles are more like country children who dance on a tiny model stage with pastoral scenery. In their Maurice Sendak version, the entire second act has a master of ceremonies, dressed as a Pasha in Turkish costume, who cracks his whip to create fantasy for Clara and her Prince.

The lighting designer will work with the production crew to position the lights so they will not be bumped by the towering Mother Ginger. As she glides onstage, a stage hand will carefully hold the curtain or the *leg,* as the narrow side curtains are called, making sure that her huge skirt doesn't get caught on a lighting boom and that the polichinelles under the skirt don't trip over one of the lighting cables taped to the stage floor.

Mother Ginger's children must be agile, alert and disciplined because they have to stay underneath the great skirt, avoiding the layers of hoops that support it while Mother is on stilts, moving sideways for her entrance and exit. A child out of place or not paying attention could trip Mother Ginger and create chaos and injury. With up to a dozen dancers in place, moving as one, carefully concealed under the massive skirt, teamwork is crucial. One wrong move and the entire monolith of Mother Ginger could fall apart or fall over.

Soon, the polichinelles burst from the under the skirt, and the high jinks of Mother Ginger and her offspring begin, to the delight of the audience. They dance simple movements, appropriate for their age and level of training,

A lock grid fly system for scenery

Many years ago, at the old Metropolitan Opera House in New York, the famous ballerina Alexandra Danilova was dancing, when, in the middle of Act One, a gel frame fell out of one of the overhead lights, hitting her on the top of her head and leaving a nasty gash. But like a true professional she continued on until a natural break in the performance allowed her to leave the stage. She swallowed some aspirin, affixed a Band-Aid where it wouldn't show, and applied an ice pack while she waited for her next cue.

A lighting tree or boom.

The role of a *Nutcracker* polichinelle (Mother Ginger's children) is generally reserved for younger, smaller children, and because of the long tradition associated with the character, the role is coveted. But today's polichinelles do not look like their ancestor, Puncinella. They're less grotesquely costumed, and the role combines a touch of magic, a bit of comedy and a hint of misbehavior, all designed to accompany the portrayal of a most memorable *Nutcracker* character—Mother Ginger!

while Mother Ginger cavorts behind them, proudly watching her charges and sometimes upstaging them with exaggerated movements. Backstage, preparations are underway for Mother Ginger to leave the stage.

"Stand by for the exit," comes the stage manager's voice over the head set that ties him to other members of the production crew.

The stage manager stands in the *prompt* corner, so named because in traditional early drama and opera, a *prompter* would feed forgotten lines to those onstage. The stage manager *calls* the show, directing the minute-by-minute operation of the production through the headset. He or she is the person responsible for making sure everyone about the stage is working together and aware of approaching curtain times. He or she will signal the orchestra conductor to enter the orchestra pit, direct the *fly* man when to change drops and the stagehands when to move the sets.

In the days before headsets things backstage were a bit more freewheeling. Hand signals, similar to those used by riggers on construction sites, were common. From the mid-seventeenth century until the late nineteenth century many stagehands had been sailors, and they fell back on whistle commands similar to what they learned while at sea to signify booms and sails flying above everyone's head. At sea the tradition is clear and long standing: only the boatswain mates, a ship's "stagehands," are permitted to whistle (it is considered bad luck if anyone else does so). In today's theater, the concept retains its impact: whistling backstage brings bad luck because it could signal someone will fly a set on stage before proper preparations are made!

The polichinelles dance playfully from the skirt of Mother Ginger.

• BALLET ENSEMBLE OF TEXAS

Arthur Leeth relates, "I remember years ago an apprentice dancer was on stilts, the little dancers under his skirt; then, inadvertently, he stepped on the hem of his skirt. We watched him fall as if it was in slow motion. There was nothing we could do, and the entire group collapsed in a heap right on stage! Later, he said he could feel all the tiny hands trying to keep him upright, even as he was pitching over."(Fortunately, it was a dress rehearsal and no one was hurt.)

109

Waltz of the Flowers

Soon, the stage fills with all the flowers of the Kingdom, led by a sparkling Dewdrop. . . .

S lowly, gracefully, the music builds as the most familiar portion of the ballet score fills the theater . . . and a *corps de ballet* of sixteen exquisitely costumed dancers move in unison onstage, heads high, arms in front and gracefully curved, legs stretched, feet pointed. They are in perfect formation, and for an instant they're immobile, like gorgeous statues. Then, in a single breath, with arms lifting, heads tilting, as if a gentle breeze wafts through the line, as if they are a row of beautiful flowers in a garden, the dancers start to waltz and turn, spinning and sliding, leaping in a vivid carousel of movement.

It is the *Waltz of the Flowers,* and it is the *Nutcracker corps de ballet* who illuminate it. *Corps* dancers, whether advanced students, trainees or apprentices, spend hours in the studio during *Nutcracker* season in class or rehearsal fine-tuning their technique and learning to work together. These dancers have the skill that ensemble choreography demands. At Pacific Northwest Ballet, for example, the *corps de ballet* for both the snow scene (see Chapter Seven) and the *Waltz of the Flowers* are advanced students from the affiliated ballet school as well as apprentices and professional dancers with the company itself. "This helps us see how the advanced students will work if we decide to take them into the company," says Artistic Director Francia Russell.

Under the usual classical ballet *syllabus,* children begin serious dance training between the ages of six and eight. They start with one or two classes per week, and by the time they reach the age of twelve, they should be in the studio four days per week. They will take a one-and-one-half hour technique class each day they are in the studio plus a separate pointe class twice a week. As they progress, they will add variations and character classes.

More advanced is the *trainee,* a member of the company who has graduated from high school and from the company's affiliated school or another studio.

Trainees work with the company professionals, take company class, dance in the *corps de ballet* but are not paid. They sign a contract and agree to a training period of one to two years during which they will be evaluated by the director, resident choreographers and ballet master to determine if they will develop and fit well in the company.

An *apprentice* is a little older than a trainee, with perhaps a year or two of experience with a small company or several years of experience in a serious college ballet program (such as Mercyhurst College in Erie, Pennsylvania, Indiana University, the University of Utah or Brigham Young University). Apprentices are chosen by audition and are usually considered a good match technically and anatomically to other company dancers. They are paid a small (sometimes a very small!) salary, and they are judged by the director and ballet master on their work ethic and ultimate fitness to be full-time professionals with the company.

Members of the *corps de ballet* make up the body of the company, and it is from here that company soloist dancers usually come. It is true that some dancers stay in the *corps* their entire careers, only occasionally dancing the coveted soloist roles. Others catch the eye of the director or ballet master early and get promoted to soloist status. From here, reaching *Principal Dancer* level is a natural next step.

For young dancers, promotion up the performance ladder is always a vibrant hope, and the demands of the *Nutcracker* ballet with its multiple performances and varied casting provide a most viable opportunity. Injuries and sickness are a daily concern, and dancers will tire from the repetitive

A delicate Dewdrop Fairy
• AMERICAN BALLET THEATRE

*Arabian Coffee—the product
of years of training*
• BALLET ENSEMBLE OF TEXAS

Rosemarie Sabovick had been dancing in the *corps de ballet* with New Jersey Ballet for five years. One day during *Nutcracker* season, the dancer performing Sugar Plum Fairy suffered an injury, then the understudy for Sugar Plum also became injured! Because Rosemary had been quietly studying the role, just in case, she was chosen, and did Sugar Plum so well that she continued to dance as Principal with New Jersey Ballet for the next fifteen years.

Rosemary Sabovick (with Michael Owen as Cavalier) in her first performance as Sugar Plum Fairy
• NEW JERSEY BALLET

performance schedule. When something happens, another dancer must be ready to fill in. Where to look for that dancer? In the *corps de ballet,* of course.

Waltz of the Flowers is the variation in which *corps* members have a strong opportunity to move up. Most *Nutcrackers* have two lead flowers as well as Dewdrop, which is a soloist role. Because all the *Waltz* dancers rehearse together, the corps members find it easy to learn lead and soloist roles.

Costumed in flowing, romantic tutus, flowers ringing carefully coiffed hair, the *corps* sways and waltzes to the buoyant, graceful music that heralds the entrance of the reappearance of Sugar Plum Fairy and her Cavalier. Every *corps* member's foot is pointed the same way, every arm lifted to the same height, every head tilted at the same angle… This moment is the culmination of the performance, the precious dessert that highlights the delicacies of the Kingdom of Sweets.

The Farewell

As the flowers move away, the moment comes that everyone has been waiting for: the Cavalier leads the exquisite Sugar Plum Fairy onstage for their memorable *pas de deux*. The Cavalier springs into a bright tarantella and Sugar Plum performs her delicate variation to the fairy-bell tones of the celesta. As the music builds to a crescendo, they pirouette across the stage to a dramatic finale.

Then, Sugar Plum calls on her subjects: Chocolate, Tea, Coffee, the
Cossacks and the Mirlitons. Each reprises a portion of their earlier dance.
You must return home now, Sugar Plum tells Clara, as she summons the sleigh.
The Nutcracker Prince gently lifts Clara onto the seat. Clara soars slowly,
gently into the air, waving a sad farewell to her new friends, floating higher
and higher. . . .

When morning comes, Clara awakens to find herself in her own bed.

It has been a beautiful dream.

The bows are worked out ahead of time and are taken in order of appearance: Chocolate, Tea, Coffee, the Russian dancers, Mirlitons, Mother Ginger (without her stilts and skirt), angels and polichinelles, the flowers (the *corps*) with Dewdrop. Finally Clara and her Prince, followed by the Sugar Plum Fairy and her Cavalier. Then the curtain closes.

Clara and her Prince bow…
• BALLET ENSEMBLE OF TEXAS

. . . and last, the Sugar Plum Fairy and her Cavalier bow to applause and cheers from the audience

• BALLET ENSEMBLE OF TEXAS

Bibliography/Videography

Books

Anderson, Jack, *The Nutcracker Book*. New York: Mayflower, 1979.

Balanchine, George and Francis Mason, *Balanchine's Festival of Ballet, Volume II*. London: W.H. Allen and Co., PLC, 1984.

Barringer, Janice and Sarah Schlesinger, *The Pointe Book, Second Edition*. Hightstown, NJ: Princeton Book Company, 2004.

Clark, Mary and Clement Crisp, *The Ballet Goer's Guide*. New York: Alfred A. Knopf, 1981.

Coe, Robert, *Dance in America*. New York: E.P. Dutton, 1985.

Danilova, Alexandra, *Choura: The Memoirs of Alexandra Danilova*. New York: Alfred A. Knopf, 1986.

Davis, Mike and Davis Hall, *The World of Ballet and Dance*. London: Hamlyn, 1973.

Fisher, Jennifer, *Nutcracker Nation*. New Haven and London: Yale University Press, 2003.

Goulden, Shirley, *The Royal Book of Ballet*. Chicago: Follett, 1962.

Gruen, John, *The World's Greatest Ballets*. New York: Harry N. Abrams, 1981.

Grant, Gail, *Technical Manual and Dictionary of Classical Ballet*. New York: Dover Publications, 1950.

Grigorovich, Yuri and Boris Poknovsky, *The Bolshoi*. New York: William Morrow and Co., 1979.

Hoffman, E.T.A, *The Nutcracker*. New York: Stewart, Tabori and Chang, 1996.

Kirstein, Lincoln, *The New York City Ballet*. New York: Alfred A. Knopf, 1973.

Krementz, Jill, *A Very Young Dancer*. New York: Alfred A. Knopf, 1976.

Mara, Thalia, *The Language of Ballet*. Hightstown, NJ: Dance Horizons, Princeton Book Company, 1987.

Meyerowitz, Joel, *George Balanchine's The Nutcracker*. Boston: Little, Brown and Company, 1993.

Money, Keith, *Pavlova, Her Life and Art*. New York: Alfred A. Knopf, 1982.

Payne, Charles, *American Ballet Theatre*. New York: Alfred A. Knopf, 1983.

Taper, Bernard, *Balanchine, A Biography*. New York: Times Books, 1984.

Shollar, Ludmilla and Anatole Vilzak, *A Ballerina Prepares*. Hightstown, NJ: Princeton Book Company, 1986.

Volkov, Solomon, *Balanchine's Tchaikovsky: Interviews with George Balanchine*. New York: Simon and Schuster, 1985.

Wiley, Roland John, *The Life and Ballets of Lev Ivanov*. Oxford, England: Clarendon Press, 1997.

Videography

American Ballet Theatre and Mikhail Baryshnikov, *The Nutcracker*. MGM/UA Home Video, 1977.

Australian Ballet, *The Nutcracker*. Kultur, 1994.

Barbie in The Nutcracker. Mattel Entertainment, 2001.

Birmingham Royal Ballet, *The Nutcracker*. BBC, Covent Garden Pioneer FSP Limited, The Royal Opera House, 1994.

Bolshoi Ballet, *The Nutcracker*. Kultur, 1978.

Kirov Ballet, *The Nutcracker*. Video Treasures, 1984.

Mark Morris, *The Hard Nut*. Elektra Nonesuch, 1992.

New York City Ballet, *George Balanchine's The Nutcracker, 1986*. Warner Bros. Family Entertainment, 1994.

Nuttiest Nutcracker, Columbia/Tristar, 2001.

The Nutcracker Prince. Warner Studios, 1999.

Pacific Northwest Ballet, *Nutcracker: The Motion Picture*. Atlantic Releasing Corporation, 1986.

Royal Ballet Covent Garden, *The Nutcracker*. Kultur, 1985.

Rudolf Nureyev with the Royal Ballet in *The Nutcracker*. Kultur, 1968.

The Dancer. First Run Features, 1994.

Vermont Ballet Theatre, *The Nutcracker*. Peter Benjamin Video Productions, 1992.